A Brief History of Thought – *Unfinished*
Essays and Poems

John Bryson AM

BROADCAST

Published by Therese O'Neill, in loving memory.

Text © Therese O'Neill, 2023
Therese O'Neill asserts the moral right to be identified as the owner of this work.
Cover portrait © Richard Leplastrier, 2023
Drawings © Richard Leplastrier, 2022, and courtesy of the State Library of New South Wales

 A catalogue record for this work is available from the National Library of Australia

ISBN: 978-0-6458440-2-3 Paperback

All rights reserved. Except as permitted under the *Australian Copyright Act 1968* (for example, fair dealing for the purposes of study, research, criticism or review) no part of this book may be reproduced, stored in a retrieval system, communicated or transmitted in any form or by any means without prior written permission from the copyright holders. All enquiries should be made to Therese O'Neill: thereseon@icloud.com

Produced by Broadcast Books, www.broadcastbooks.com.au
Cover design by Nada Backovic, www.nadabackovic.com
Text design and typeset in 12.5pt Sabon by Nada Backovic
Proofread by Puddingburn Publishing Services
Printed by Ingram Spark

Every effort has been made to trace accurate ownership of copyrighted text used in this book. Errors or omissions will be corrected in subsequent editions, provided notification is sent to Therese O'Neill, thereseon@icloud.com

Forewords

Therese O'Neill

John's journey into *A Brief History of Thought* began in around 2015. It excited him to commit to the process and see where it would take him. Being a man of great stamina and inexhaustible will, John didn't regard the project as daunting, but rather it energised him.

His dream was to complete it and have it published. I watched and celebrated every step of the way. Daily progress was recounted over a glass of wine. As John moved deeper into the writing, he asked me to promise that I would have it published should anything happen to him. Although, his zest for life was such that he believed he would live to be a hundred.

I assured him my project was to keep him alive until his work was published.

While John was writing and researching this collection, he was able to combine that passion with his daily routine and myriad of hobbies. One such hobby was cooking and producing a new dish or sauce; sharing it with our friends totally fulfilled him.

When John became ill, I questioned my ability to carry out his wish to publish this book. He nominated a few of his very dear friends who would support me. While there were many challenges along the way, I made it through and now with a heavy heart I can say:

Your wish fulfilled, my love, my promise kept.

Therese
Lovett Bay, Pittwater

Paolo Totaro AM

This is a collection of so far unpublished works that John Bryson promised his wife Therese would be part of his legacy. He was still well then, but soon he would be losing some of the gifts for which he was distinguished: speech and writing.

His last thoughts were put into this book.

John was gifted. His masterpiece, *Evil Angels*, is now among those books through which Australian literature is known in the world.

He was indeed one of the finest wordsmiths in the country. I suspect, though, that John would have refused to use these words to describe himself.

As a barrister, John recognised the power of words. He was trained to distil the arguments and to discern the real thing.

Words, in his hands, had to lose as much as possible all the signifiers that weren't essential to the purpose of a given phrase. When writing, he would eliminate any excesses. Like Paul Klee, one of the first abstract painters to draw a tree subtracted from all non-essential elements for its identification as a tree – one species and not another, at some time of the day and light condition and not another. Thereby, leaving the tree in its truest form. John, similarly, spent hours reducing the words until he got to their essence.

For most people, this would require an effort and probably did so for John too.

Integritas, *consonantia* and *clarita*s: his style was to me, like no other living Australian author.

John spent the last years of his life grappling with the notion of consciousness – and the loss of it.

In conversation, John and I discussed whether the lack of consciousness was not a contradiction; that is, to have consciousness about the loss of consciousness. And I remember him saying that the quantity of consciousness found in a person's discourse was a diagnostic tool sometimes defining that person's capacity to discern and argue.

He had a gift and he used it well.

Paolo

Margot Hutcheson

John wrote, refined and combined the essays and poems in this collection over several years, crafting into them his thoughts on consciousness, life, history, the universe, everything. They reflect his lifelong interest in the changing nature of humans throughout time.

It was a subject John spent his life researching, as a criminal barrister, a writer, a father, a mentor, a friend and a truly *human* human being.

Here he lays out and encapsulates his findings for all to read.

As he was dying, John tasked Therese O'Neill, his beloved spouse, to publish this work.

Her persistence is why you are able to read this book now.

Margot

Richard Leplastrier AO

John Noel Bryson's nickname was The Chief.

He was a poet, storyteller, rally-car driver, high-end racing sailor and rower, nature lover and a practising criminal barrister through to his middle years. A fighter for justice and the fair go.

We were close friends and talked often and at length. I asked him once why he stopped practising law. His answer was both immediate and shocking … 'Because every criminal barrister I knew, became a criminal.'

So his intellectual pendulum swung towards his greatest love, the Arts. *A Brief History of Thought* is his last work, his final case. In it, he puts the case for the power of philosophy and the Arts, through history. To overturn the dead hand of conservatism and greed. It is his final cross-examination, his ultimate summing up.

Richard

Contents

John's essays	1
Time is in no hurry	3
In the 500 or more million years	7
An organism	11
Darwin	13
The stone ruins	21
If we think of works of the imagination	23
The Anglican Church	25
Difficult	29
To assume language is a necessary condition	31
Writing made its mark	35
At Mount Sinai	39
Planning for the building of large structures	41
Culture is the personality of a people	43
A character	47
Fine character performances	53
And, magically now, the first appearance of painted portraits	57
Under permissive Buddhism	59

The sudden appearance in Japan of figures	63
The reach of song to share emotions	65
Dance began	69
Rhythm, repetition and attractive conjunctions of sounds	71
Music is the purest fiction now	75
The function of the artistries	79
In fear of a predatory world	83
The Greeks in their Classical era	87
An acquired urge	89
No need of gods	91
Repeating the same mistake	93
Contagious life	95
The soul and consciousness	97
Hard problems abound	101
Cooperation as a civil method	109
Spectacular change is with us now	113
A function of every life	117
With the influences directing human development	121
Consciousness	123
Slavery continues	127
Uncoupling morality from the gods	131
A secular morality	133
Development of abstract thought	137
A contemporary search for a secular morality	141

Evolutionary paths to a secular ethic	143
Absence of evolutionary theory	147
One might have expected a secular society	149
The algorithm	151
References	155
John's poems	*161*
Notes on the poems	163
An age of unsteady progress	164
For Paolo Totaro	164
For John Bryson	165
On greater age	166
Were we shearwaters, a meridian	167
Ko Tupapaku Tapu, Lying in state	168
William John O'Meally, flogged	169
Painting fish	170
This fallen leaf	171
From a voyage	172
Of Waratah Bay	173
September and September	174
16th June 2014, Iraq	175
Hatchlings	176
Whakamarumaru	177
An exorcism	177
Even beyond life	178
Epilogue	179
About the drawings	181

Forest 4/8
RLP

Forest. 5/8
RLP

Forest 6/8
RLP

John's essays

Time is in no hurry

Charles Darwin, travelling through the 1830s with the *Beagle*, saw earthly formations that clearly were the result of forces sometimes swift, sometimes imperceptibly slow. Lands were drowned by oceans, littorals elevated to high altitude. He found marine fossils on mountainsides. His was an inquiry begun in 1770 by the Scot James Hutton, carried further by the inquisitive friends Humboldt and Goethe in a search for 'the great harmonies of nature'. Humboldt was trained in geology. Darwin carried a copy of Humboldt's *Personal Narrative* on the *Beagle* voyages. This capacity with geology gave Darwin an advantage in dealing with deep time: 'the lapse of time has been so great as to be utterly inappreciable by the human intellect'.[1]

The very first release of energy, anywhere or anytime, so most physicists believe, was the Big Bang, which is still in train as we speak and without which

---

[1] Charles Darwin, Chapter 14: 'Recapitulation and Conclusion', *On the Origin of Species*, 1859.

gravity on the surface of our spinning globe wouldn't be feasible. The mother of all explosions, indeed the mother of all things, cannot be placed in the time continuum we are used to, but in the awkward first stage, because it began time, as it began space.

So, from a state of nothing came the explosion that created matter and created energy. The sudden existence of matter begat volume, which is a measurement of matter, which begat space. The sudden existence of energy begat movement, which begat time, which is a measurement of movement. So began space/time.

Dr Katie Mack describes the earliest phase of creation, now called the 'Electroweak Era', as very brief: 'Experiments that produce electroweak interactions are giving us a glimpse of the processes within the first trillionth of a second of the Universe.'[2]

Alternatively, if we hold to the First Law of Thermodynamics, energy cannot be created or destroyed, so has existed always. Energy and volume and mass were then in a form which current science cannot explain.

Development toward the possibility of life somewhere in the cooling Earth is then so gradual no word in our language conveys it. Changes in matter and energy happen in nano-instants and so ceaselessly as to invite use of the word 'forever'. Turbulence of this magnitude does not allow any state of stability to

---

2   Katie Mack, 'Recreating the beginning of time', *Cosmos*, 29 June 2015.

establish easily, but some matter loses energy enough to cool and become sufficiently consistent of form to allow lasting changes in its structure. Developing elements and compounds and complex molecules so to produce at least one world with an atmosphere which is so shallow that the tallest mountains poke through it into the stratosphere. Other than tiny space flotsam, its biosphere is a closed energy system, dependent on the entry of sunlight. Whenever creation was, within the concept of time we now use, the best science can do is approximate the point at which planet Earth might be said to have begun, at about 4.6 billion years ago.

When the mantle had become a solid, the Earth's chemical structure was mineral, defined by the components of physics we see as heat and the four forces: gravitational, electromagnetic with the two nuclear. Preparing for life with the first simple cells required waiting a billion years. For a development into bacteria capable of photosynthesis another 200 million years; 1.4 billion years more to complex cells; 1800 million years further for sexual reproduction to replace division; 1600 million years later saw simple animals; 150 million years on to water-form life; 125 million years to plants on the land; 95 million years to amphibians; 160 million to mammals; 140 million to primates; and another 47 million years to the first *Homo*. *Homo habilis* developed an opposable thumb, a larynx necessary for speech and an interest in tools. Anatomically, modern humans appeared about 200,000 years before the date on today's newspaper.

In the 500 or more million years

In the 500 or more million years following the development of land-based plants, various species randomly achieved methods of propagation by attraction of pollinators, using shape, colour and odour attractive to useful visitors. The arrival of hominids, then, particularly after the selection of techniques known as the agricultural revolution, brought enormous change in successful plant species.

An excursion to one of today's local produce markets illustrates the changes in evolutionary methodology enabled by the appearance of sophisticated abstract thought in humankind, beginning in Neolithic times. Previously, all plants that propagated sexually, rather than by division or physical extension, made their flowers and fruit attractive to insects and animals, so to use the motion of insects for cross pollination, and for birds and animals to carry seeds far.

Enabled by the Neolithic revolution, those plants producing fruit or vegetables endeared to human taste, nutrition or aesthetic are now cultivated in communities around the globe, wherever climate and nutrients can be tamed to permit. Successful species in the competition for life are no longer those that happen on a genetic development which makes for advantage over competitors, and therefore prosper, but those which attract the efforts of humankind to extend their production.

Admirers of tulip production globally, tulip mania having begun in the Netherlands and been encouraged by Rembrandt, will have little thought for the Australian Spider Orchid declared extinct newly at the time of writing. Fruits are currently at the centre of propagation efforts. Bananas top the global consumption list, most now produced in India, the Southern Americas and China. In many of the poorer countries, bananas are the staple. Bananas are commonly propagated by the physical transplant of shoots, allowing consumption of all fruits, rather than propagation by fruit fall. So have some plant species improved on random evolution.

So with beasts. The Maasai peoples of Kenya and Tanganyika, who moved south from the Nile during the 15th century, bringing their herds of Zebu cattle, had developed techniques of assisted fertilisation for their cows. Elsewhere, producers of edible flesh looked to artificial insemination and, later, inoculation so to maintain high production. These species were benefiting from human management.

Has a species ever completed the transition from the wild to take advantage of human management?

A contender for early defection by a species from the natural mechanism for evolutionary success, which is random change and selection, in favour of advantage provided by the intervention of humankind, is the saffron flower *Crocus sativus*. Saffron threads, the stigma, used as a spice and dye, prized in several regions of the world over thousands of years, were noted in hieroglyphs held by the Royal Library of Ashurbanipal from the Assyrian Bronze Age collapse. Ninety per cent of world production is currently in Iran. The crocus is propagated by hand, the corms separated and replanted. The threads command US$14,000 per kilo in the West. *Crocus sativus* is no longer known in the wild.

The Neolithic revolution, sometimes called the first agricultural revolution, around 10,000 years before the common era, prepared the way for a momentum to replace the primordial forms of regeneration which perpetuated life, as described by Darwin, Wallace and Huxley. Thereby replacing it with radical and direct methods of management.

So does sophisticated abstract thought overpower the established order, as some species hitch their ride with humankind, while others fail? This movement in management practice flagged the possibility that humankind has moved the biological world from the Darwinian observation of random change, selection, success or failure, into systems chosen by abstractions, intellectual vessels, ideas. Darwinian evolution may be no more. Breeders of plants and animals have practised genetic influence since well before Mendel. Humankind is changing itself and the species around it, as ecologists warn.

An organism

An organism, perhaps a single cell, which perceives the conditions for survival, including sustenance and propagation, may be said to have elementary consciousness. The first made its appearance a little earlier than 3.5 billion years ago. Many millions of years of life passed by until single-celled microbes began communicating with signals and cooperating to form complexities, then acting together as if a single unit. Activity made possible because of some capacity for rudimentary choice.

By the lifetime of any reader of this, the number of living cells on Earth is inexpressible to human thought. By Richard Dawkins' count in *The Selfish Gene*: 'Taking just insects alone, the number of living species has been estimated at around three million, and the number of individual insects may be a million million million.'

The cooperative of living cells constructing a human body is vast enough to be best expressed by scientists with an exponent, of which 10^{13} is a current favourite. Human population in the year 1800 CE was 1 billion, in the year of writing this the figure has passed 7 billion and, if the trajectory holds, by the year 2100 may be 16 billion. In Dawkins' view, the territories we should recognise as hosts to living cells include all the animal and plant kingdoms, and additionally viruses to which cells are the host, and that outnumber all other organisms. All of them conscious.

A brain is not necessary to consciousness in animals. Worms and many sea creatures are capable of gregarious behaviour and of survival manoeuvres without brains, by allowing simple neural networks of a quite different order. Beyond elementary cognition and simple reaction, a brain is the finest biological instrument we know of in the organisation of cognition, information storage, retrieval, selection and judgement. Leaps in hominin brain size are remarkable from *H. habilis*, beginning an association with tools, around 2.5 million years ago, through each succession, to our own species beginning 200,000 years ago.

Large brained hominids spread to Asia and Southern Europe, then died out. Modern humans from Africa routed south to Asia, Australia, north through the Middle East and, about 15,000 years ago, to the Americas. Social patterns were established, myriad languages, information about the natural world, beliefs about the supernatural.

Darwin

Darwin, in *On the Origin of Species,* summarises the progression of natural selection:

> Growth with Reproduction; Inheritance which is almost implied by Reproduction; Variability from the indirect and direct action of the external conditions of life and from use and disuse; a Ratio of Increase so high as to lead to a Struggle for Life, and as a consequence to Natural Selection entailing Divergence of Character and Extinction of less-improved forms.

He was considering the development and survival of biological beings. He seems not to have considered how natural selection may play its part in the development and survival of abstract constructs, institutions, arrangements, complexes, indeed ideas.

With this paragraph in *Origin* he is close:

> If we suppose any habitual act to become inherited – and I think it can be shown that this does sometimes happen – then the resemblance between what originally was a habit and an instinct becomes so close as not to be distinguished. If Mozart, instead of playing the pianoforte at three years old with wonderfully little practice, had played a tune with no practice at all, he might truly be said to have done so instinctively. But it would be the most serious error to suppose that the greatest number of instincts have been acquired by habit in one generation, and then transmitted by inheritance to succeeding generations.

Darwin focuses his work on the modification of a devised system, a contrived complex we explain as instinct, by the principles of natural selection. And: 'As modifications of corporeal structure arise from, and are increased by, use or habit, and are diminished or lost by disuse, so I do not doubt it has been with instincts.'

Instinctive behaviour in many primitive species – behaviour which is inherited within the genetic system – seems more extensive than in the newborn human. With a large but yet to be informed brain, the baby has a pattern of responses supporting maintenance of breathing and noisy reaction to hunger and other pain. Physiologists and psychologists could point to more of these patterned responses, and their indelibility. Clearly a human organism will develop a vaster amount of behavioural capacity by conditioning than by a pattern in the mould. Thus providing for greater diversity of behavioural propensities in its lifetime, and so greater range of novelty on which natural selection can make its pitiless choice.

All is gradual, Darwin reminds us: 'The canon of *Natura non facit saltum* (Nature makes no leaps, i.e., is gradual) applies with almost equal force to instincts as to bodily organs.'

Given our ease and facility now with the construct, and the virtual, we might readily identify a belief, a religion, a church, as an institution subject to evolutionary forces and to natural selection. Darwin was nervous of the responses to his theory by the churches. His mother had been Unitarian, he studied at Christ's College, he married within the Church, and his wife feared his heresies might separate them in the afterlife.

Most of those around him attempted to explain variations found in fossils, within the one species of animal, by a divine design in which members of a species were assembled with these differences in place at the instant of creation. Darwin's vision was of instability of species. His focus was on inherited accidental variations perpetuated by success in the struggle for life.

Darwin's model for the continued existence of a species relied on the availability to it of variations, some of them advantageous, destined to be successful. He himself, with the publication of *Origin* then *The Descent of Man*, was providing variations to the advantage of a complex, of an institution, his Church of England.

During 1860, a year after publication of *Origin*, 11,000 Anglican clergy signed a declaration of adherence to biblical creationism. The same year Bishop Wilberforce and Thomas Huxley famously debated evolutionism at Oxford to a vast audience. Playing to ridicule, the bishop asked Huxley whom did he claim to be descended from – a monkey, his grandmother or his grandfather? Huxley is reported to have replied: 'I am not ashamed to have a monkey as an ancestor, but I would be ashamed to be connected to a man who used great gifts to obscure a truth.' In the uproar that followed, Lady Brewster fainted and was carried out. This is her sole appearance in the histories.

Providing a variation in Anglican orthodoxy, to favour adjusting Anglican belief in the divine method to keep step with scientific knowledge, was becoming a consequence of Darwinian theory. Darwin had himself provided this variation which might be useful to a church, as an institution, for survival advantage. Most of Darwin's contemporary admirers took a syncretic course with his theories, accepting him as explaining the divine method.

By his death in 1882, Darwin's evolutionism had effected enough variation in Anglican thought as to give him an acceptance for burial in Westminster Abbey. In 1896 a Darwinian supporter, Frederick Temple, became Archbishop of Canterbury. Through the 1950s the syncretistic Jesuit Pierre Teilhard de Chardin strove to provide a form in which evolutionary Darwinism might become acceptable to Catholic doctrine, but his *Le Phenomene Humain* and other works were banned. By 2005 the then Archbishop of Canterbury and the Bishop of Leicester were able to praise Darwin, although without endorsing pure evolutionism. Most clergy seem happy enough to allow an evolutionism as clarifying divine method.

A permitted variation in belief is not common among the Mesopotamian religions. The Vatican would refuse its discussion until the 1950s, when Pope Pius XII issued *Humani Generis*, holding to 'divinely communicated truth'. Hassidic Jews hold to the Torah, while Progressives do not, and in part of Islam, belief in evolution is an apostasy punishable only by death.

Darwin saw variations were necessary, in biology, for the continuation of a species. Also, for the patterns of behaviour which are instinctual, so as to permit improvement in the ability to survive against competition. In the patterns of behaviour which are not laid down in the genes, but are conceptual, fictions contrived and passed on as institutions, we might expect a similar requirement for survival against competition.

Building a theory of evolution that would become his *Origin*, Darwin observed similarities between certain biological forms, which others in the natural sciences typically ascribed to divine arrangement. Darwin's great step was beyond the recognition of similarities, to the primacy of variations over vast periods of time. Most of his antagonists held to biblical time. One hundred and fifty years after Darwin, much human intellect finds biblical time more to its taste.

Without an understanding of deep time, a grasp of the principles of evolution is not possible. Persistence of biblical time was Darwin's opponent. Peter Watson, in *Ideas*, records belief in biblical time as:

> For example, from Creation to the birth of Abraham there are 1946 years according to the Jewish Hebrew text, 2247 years according to the Samaritan Hebrew text, and 3412 according to the Septuagint. 3761 BC is now the date preferred for the Creation.[3]

The published chronologies, the 'timelines' of world history, choose to begin at around 4000 BCE. The more popular begin there in reverence to biblical time, or because a recognition of universal time is impracticable for them. So, they typically ascribe approximately one metre of horizontal diagram to the

---

3   Peter Watson, *Ideas: A History of Thought and Invention, from Fire to Freud*, Harper Perennial, 2006.

events of each millennium. The vastness of biblical distortion is illustrated by comparison with universal proportion. A page in universal time marking the arrival of the first anatomically modern humans should be placed 200 kilometres to the left of biblical page one, and a page representing the beginning of our universe on a line 4.5 million kilometres further, the distance between Earth and our moon, times ten.

The *New Yorker*'s John McPhee was wandering the eastern coast of the USA with geologist Kenneth Deffeyes, 120 years after Darwin wrote of 'the lapse of time' required by earthly evolution. Marvelling at the geological progressions, McPhee taking notes for *Basin and Range*, wrote:

> Numbers do not seem to work well with regard to deep time. Any number above a couple of thousand years – fifty thousand, fifty million – will, with nearly equal effect, awe the imagination to the point of paralysis.[4]

---

4   John McPhee, *Basin and Range*, Macmillan, 1982.

The stone ruins

The stone ruins at Gobekli Tepe in Anatolian Turkey are the earliest known ritual structure, built about 12,000 years ago. Late Stone Age, so pre-Neolithic, it was a social centre for a hunter–gatherer community, not yet agricultural. Many anthropologists regard this building as holding the earliest evidence of a priestly caste.

Our large brain creatures had begun 'mentalising', to use Robin Dunbar's term,[5] in common everywhere, thinking of ourselves as folk striving to understand the circumstances in which we live, how best to survive in a predatory world and, obsessively, of our creation and an afterlife. We had begun to think beyond the items and the happenings in the natural world, to the virtual, the imagined, the construct, as are found in religion. Almost universally, religions proposed a pantheon of gods with dissimilar influence, often a dominant god with powers of creation always at war with an adversarial god, and a population of lesser demons and angels. The correct rituals might bring

---

5 Robin Dunbar, et al., 'Higher-order mentalising and executive functioning', *Personality and Individual Differences*, volume 86, November 2015, pp 6–14.

favour, protection, intercession and almost universally, fortunate crops and quarry.

Nicholas Wade supposes a purpose for religions as a civilising force, in *The Faith Instinct*, encouraging sociality, group tolerance and cooperation. This is a fair assessment of its possible effect, its result within a religion, but does not help to explain cause.

Monotheism is of recent origin. A purest form seems to be Sikh, begun by Guru Nanak from a Hindu family, in around the year 1499 CE. Zoroaster in Iran during the 6th century BCE simplified the Persian religion to one dominant god, Ahura Mazda, ruling above two opposing spiritual forces, Spenta Mainyu against Angra Mainyu, a spirit for good and truth, battling a spirit for chaos and fraudulence.

The influence of Zoroaster is seen in subsequent Judaism, Christianity and Islam, in which the Divine Being presides over the battles between good and evil, influenced by angels, and the demons following a Satanic Being. Buddhism is non-theistic. In Africa, many gods were summoned for vengeance and protection, in the Pacific, for navigation. The third largest world religion, Hinduism, offers *dramatis personae* for worship as an open list, and does not preclude atheism. Gods with specialised duties, and the spirits of ancestors in afterlife, flicker as candles in countless grottoes in villages and along forest paths throughout China.

If we think of works of the imagination

If we think of works of the imagination as constructive fictions, likely this will bring to mind Vladimir Nabokov's lines in *Lectures on Literature*: 'literature was born on the day when a boy came crying "wolf, wolf" and there was no wolf' and then, 'Literature is invention. Fiction is fiction.'[6] This is a charming allusion to powers of imagination, although the beginnings he describes cannot be true as it is itself an invention to distance truthfulness from his love of imaginative leaps and their possibilities.

In search of a more primal imaginative reach, we might recall behaviour beyond humankind: a pride of female lions pack hunting and clearly imagining the possible escape routes for their quarry; birds using twigs as tools; dolphins together herding great clouds of sardines; a thousand starlings in enraptured flight

---

6   Vladimir Nabokov, *Lectures on Literature*, Harcourt Brace Jovanovich, 1980.

folding the vast flock like a twirling veil. Imagination is in play here, in early form, the condition precedent for any development beyond the naturally occurring world, the propensities.

The Anglican Church

The Anglican Church, receiving a variation successful for survival, provided by Darwin himself, is faring better than most. Those religions that hold to invariable dogma because it is sacred, cannot vary so cannot improve, presenting themselves as ultimate, therefore perfect. They do not obey the progression of natural selection, so may find difficulty surviving against competitors. These justify the category: primitive.

Ancient religions, about which we have some information, and which became extinct in the Mediterranean and the Middle East, included some spectacular failures, if we judge them on the vastness of their deserting populations. The Egyptian deities, Sun God Ra, Earth God Geb and their families, lost their following to Pharaoh worship, the deification of rulers. Only the goddess Isis survived in pockets anywhere, perhaps because of her powers of healing the sick. Ancient Semitic polytheism was replaced by Abraham's belief in the one god, then called El.

The Hellenistic syncretic religious system, carried through a millennium from Alexander the Great to

Constantine, was then to be gradually replaced with Christianity for its 54 million people.

Drawing conclusions about the nature of change in prehistoric religions calls on a daunting amount of assumption, but the rate of change might be judged using our knowledge of behaviour in contemporary peoples. Kept remote from each other by terrain, consider the tribes of Papua New Guinea, with a population of around 5.5 million, speaking 800 languages or dialects extending over sixty language groups, reflecting the waves of past immigration over 40,000 or 50,000 years. They were separated by terrain so difficult to penetrate as to keep separate a tribe in one valley from a tribe in the next valley for thousands of years. They practised animism commonly, but differently, from tribe to tribe; sacred and magical places were determined by locality, very often mountaintops and waterfalls. Most relied on the power of ancestor spirits, and magicians and shamans were considered persuasive authority. Christian missionaries complained of difficulty in converting these people, partly because these faiths had been fixed, they believed, since time immemorial. As was their distrust of strangers.

For many in 20th century Papua New Guinea, a new variation in Christianity, never before recorded, was decisive in conversion. The conventional preachers described Jesus as a personal god, a path to the rewards of salvation and everlasting life. Meanwhile those to be converted were assessing the personal wealth of Christians: money, clothing, motor vehicles, aircraft, and stories of the new seaports where huge vessels docked bringing goods of astonishing richness, a supply without end therefore, aligning a Christian faith with Christian wealth. The conclusion was compelling: join the faithful and Jesus will dispatch shiploads of goods in reward. So began the Cargo Cults of New Guinea, well described by anthropologist Peter Lawrence in *Road Belong Cargo*.

Two of the most recently created religious institutions rely on variations to do with the recognition of aliens.

The Church of Scientology, launched by science-fiction writer L. Ron Hubbard in 1952 in New Jersey, USA, did not begin as an offshoot of any theist institution, but as an extension of the practice of science fiction. Its important variation was to present the invasion of Earth by aliens from space as true. The aliens arrived in spaceships shaped much like DC3s, hid in mountain tunnels they then sealed with rock, and passed among us, perhaps for thousands of years.

Li Hongzhi, the messianic creator of Falun Gong, launched his religion in China in 1992, as a variation of Taoist Qi Gong tradition, spiritual cultivation by thought and movement, together with the Buddhist circle emblem Falun. Riding the Qi Gong tradition, it became instantly popular with many millions of Chinese practising its morality and exercise disciplines. Chinese leaders classed it a moral heresy because it taught disengagement from politics, and they currently attempt its eradication. In an interview with *Time*

Magazine, Li described his cultivation practice as a process converting mortals to a divine class, to out-manoeuver evil aliens from other planets who control human thought, and who will inhabit human cadavers, so to take over the world, 'and in the end to replace human beings'.[7]

Li has moved to New York perhaps in response to the urge in America to embrace religious belief.

---

7   William Dowell, 'Interview with Li Hongzhi', *Time Magazine*, 10 May 1999.

Difficult

Difficult, perhaps impossible, searching through humankind, to find a society in which governance began without a religious hierarchy. Alongside early religions developed institutions of authority, most likely by way of a variation giving useful prominence to a warrior class. A symbiosis seems to have established early, the priestly caste anointing the warrior caste with godly status, as in pre- Christian Rome, then through Christian Western Europe, Shinto Japan, early China, ancient Egypt. In Islam the warriors yield to the Imams, in return for paradise after life, a favourite incentive of diverse gods everywhere.

To assume language is a necessary condition

To assume language is a necessary condition precedent for abstract construction is attractive were it not for examples such as the social behaviour of primates, or the courting performances of displaying birds, or for an Australian chough, which is the one bird known to take slaves as it does for foraging food, described by biologist Tim Low in *Where Song Began*.

Transfer of knowledge, of information, of instruction, before the development of language, most anthropologists agree, must have used example, attended by sounds and gestures of approval or not, where needs arose beyond the instinctual programs. We watch the predatory mammals and birds particularly, encouraging their young, the large cats and bears with tumbling cubs come to mind. Observing fish and insects for instructive behaviour is difficult, and perhaps these actions are unlearned and instinctive until, say, a new pattern of food availability tells them otherwise. Robin

Dunbar, in an aside, writes 'we are, after all, the only living species with a language',[8] which is a view we might be slow to accept until we are fluent in the sound signals we hear from whales and dolphins. We know bees and some ants tell one another of food sources and perhaps nesting nooks by way of choreography, which we yet cannot translate.

Then 'possibly the most momentous stage in history' perhaps around 400,000 or so years ago, described at Queens University, Toronto by its Professor Merlin Donald,[9] the progression in *Homo erectus* to mimetic performance in human communication. This has been defined by Peter Watson[10] as 'intentional mime and imitation, facial expression, mimicry of sounds, gestures', which 'allowed for intentionality, creativity, reference, coordination and, perhaps above all, pedagogy, the acculturation of the young'. Humankind was beginning to teach one another about empirical experiences, an extension of consciousness in both the instructor and the tyro, each to embrace something of the mind of the other.

---

8   Robin Dunbar (ed) et al., *Lucy to Language: The Benchmark Papers*, Oxford University Press, 2014.

9   Merlin Donald, *Origins of the Modern Mind: Three stages in the evolution of culture and cognition*, Harvard University Press, 1991.

10 Peter Watson, *Ideas: A History of Thought and Invention, from Fire to Freud*, Harper Perennial, 2006.

We assume often-used sounds hardened into words. Anthropologists Morten Christianson and Simon Kirby have described the early evolution of language as 'the hardest problem in science'.[11]

The linguists' language trees offer some evidence of the conception of languages. They do not help with chronology, with timing, but do suggest locations. So we are not surprised to find many related languages in the world's most populated regions. Exceptionally, Basque has no known relatives, perhaps reflecting their preferred seclusion, later justified by General Franco's attempts at genocide. Papua New Guinea provides a surprise, with many hundreds of languages, including three spread over 1500 speakers, the effect of isolation imposed by the terrain. The very ancient 'click' languages of southern Africa so bemused invading English and Dutch they concluded the Bantu used no language but clicked at each other like insects. One of these, Xhosa, is the most widely distributed language in southern Africa, and was the first language of Nelson Mandela, victor over the British and the Dutch.

---

11 Morten H. Christiansen and Simon Kirby (eds), *Language Evolution*, Oxford University Press, 2003.

Writing made its mark

Writing made its mark perhaps 150,000 years after the development of language, or more than 7000 generations. Peter Watson is fond of calling its signifiers 'Artificial Memory Systems, and that, after all, is what writing is'.[12] This is true, but it is not all. Writing also made information transmissible, over distance and beyond lifetimes. Early on it was annexed, as a tool of authority, by the priestly caste, permitted to interpret true meanings for the subject class.

Scholars at the Schøyen Collection in Norway attribute the first symbols to Australian cave and rock painters, 40,000 to 50,000 years ago, showing 'Numbers and counting began before continuous writing'. The first colonising period for Australia is put at 40,000 to 50,000 years BCE, the early Stone Age. 'With the earliest rock carvings and painting, the cylcons represent the earliest form of communication

---

12 Peter Watson, *Ideas: A History of Thought and Invention, from Fire to Freud*, Harper Perennial, 2006.

and art, and they represent the earliest religion still observed.'[13]

The earliest cylcon found, a sandstone oval, is marked with three series of regular lines, 12 + 9 + 14, near Bourke in New South Wales, 'possibly recording the number of young men to pass the initiation rituals to manhood of the Australian people "Bora"'. At best estimate, the message from this Elder at an ancient ceremony has travelled 20,000 years to its present reader.

The Collection lists the earliest known item of continuous writing as a Sumerian Receipt on a clay tablet recording 'Receipt of unnamed objects by 5 named persons', in pictographic script, dated about 3200 years BC. Another tablet found nearby records 'an account of male and female slaves' carrying ostriches and wine.

Before literacy, information was recorded and passed on by chants, by song and poetry, where rhythm, tone and rhyme could provide an aide memoire. In the Middle East the cuneiform, wedge-shaped drawings, began to include codes that used a manner of pictorial pun to make a sentence, selecting a shape representing a sound with two different meanings, which we now call homonyms, in modern English. Say 'cricket' for an insect and a game, leaving the choice of appropriate meaning to the reader. Some linguists suggest this was,

---

13 See: www.historyofinformation.com/detail.php?entryid=5 and www.schoyencollection.com/23-religions/living-religions/23-9-australian-aborigne

in several societies, the path writing took to become phonetic.

In an atonal language the number of sounds available is few, the development of words with multiple meanings is high, the listener or the reader must choose according to context. In a tonal language the availability of discrete sounds is high, fewer words have multiple meanings. Is this why Chinese held to a pictorial script? In its modern lifetime with Hanyu Pinyin, writing in Mandarin is taking the Latin phonetic path.

French linguist Jesuit Alexandre de Rhodes in the 17th century augmented a phonetic alphabet of 29 characters and tonal punctuation to service Vietnamese, the quoc ngu, to replace characters, giving it a three-century phonetic advantage over Chinese.

Writing made us its gift of amusing foibles, of which four come readily to mind: graffiti and crossword puzzles in the West, fortune cookies in China, and in Vietnam the bamboo shades called Poetry Hats, in which favourite lines from poems are written on the underside of the wide brim for reading when cocked a little forward.

At Mount Sinai

At Mount Sinai Moses smashed the first two tablets of the Ten Commandments in a fit of anger in 1400 years BCE, biblical time. His god, written as YHWH in a language yet without vowels, duplicated them with his writing finger, for the early Israelites, using an ancient Hebrew that is probably the language we call Canaanite Semitic. If found, the tablets will represent the earliest writings in this language, since present evidence puts the earliest attested Hebrew writing at the 10th century BCE. By the time of Moses' conversation with YHWH, writing had been created, so ancient Egyptians believed, in lands not far away, by the deity Thoth, scribe to the higher gods, also inventor of science. A being often depicted in human form but with the head of an ibis, writer of *The Book of the Dead*, appearing in the crypts of the pyramids.

Developments in writing in Mesopotamia around 3200 BCE, about the same time in India, 1500 years later in Mesoamerica, moved custodianship of scripture from the poets and chanters to the scribes. And more easily available then for study and interpretation, so beginning the rise of a liturgical lawyer class.

A recording system that fixes sacred teachings unalterably in time and knowledge performs a holy duty in the major religions. Fixed instruction expressed in a fixed voice, but its permanency relies on human language in which semantic signifiers change, words change, over time and usage. A common method in defence of a one-true-belief is to punish deviation with death. Lawyerly priests, rabbis, gurus, mullahs, continue to argue amongst themselves about the purity of record, about interpretation, about apostasy and heresy. Judaism diffused into nearly twenty movements or sects, Christianity 41,000 denominations, Islam yet short of the seventy-three sects predicted by the Prophet Mohammad now around eighteen, Buddhism into merely two or three, and Hindu without meaningful numbers. All depending on definition, all tending toward a maxim: In humankind we believe as we wish to believe.

    YHWH and other deities will have been curiously watching the development of writing the languages of humankind in diverse centres of population. In Mesoamerica the Mayan people attributed the creation of writing to Itzamna, who was also the creator of the world and, on modern calculations, this event occurred about 500 years BCE. The Chinese were not magically minded about the appearance of writing, created by Ts'ang Cheih, a learned courtier to Emperor Huangdi, around 2500 BCE. The Yellow Emperor, whom artists often drew in ink drawings on golden shantung, was traditionally responsible for the beginning of Chinese civilisation, but perhaps mythical.

Planning for the building of large structures

Planning for the building of large structures before writing and literacy raises intriguing speculation about the then transmissibility of calculations, measurement, necessary forces, the order of effort, foundation strength, gravitational effect on planes, tilting moment. Instructions from the ancient architects to their builders must have used oral and diagrammatic directions. Diagrams have either perished or remain untranslatable.

Turkey's Gobekli Tepe, the complex religious sanctuary in praise of the Annunaki deities of the age, was begun around 9000 years BCE, a building designed to stand 15 metres tall, the complex 300 metres in diameter, from stone blocks some of 50 tonnes, with sixteen pillars 7 metres tall.

Nearly as ancient, perhaps from 8000 years ago, in Australia's Lake Conder, the Gunditjmara people built an intricate system of channels and ponds over 75 square kilometres, alongside a stone village where foundations still lie, farming eels they then smoked and traded. Principles of hydrology had entered their lore.

Graves, tombs and fortifications are common ancient structures through those regions which put to good use knowledge from their Stone Ages, Europe, the Middle East, and the Americas. Designs for simple blocks of stone, construction techniques suited to oral and diagrammatic transmission, carrying sometimes beyond many generations. The stone city in Peru's Rio Casma Valley was begun by Incas 5600 years ago, its Sechin Bajo temple added 2000 years later, so requiring builders over thirty to forty lifetimes for building, maintenance and replacements. Its ruins were rediscovered during the 1990s.

The burial ground in Wiltshire in the UK, Stonehenge, carried ritual structures since 8000 BCE. Its community erected headstones of bluestone over its graves. About 2600 BCE they began the raising of monoliths, continuing rearrangements for the next thousand years, say fifty generations.

Pyramid construction times were fleeting by comparison because of the large populations. The Great Pyramid of Giza was planned with a diagram of full size, modern Egyptologists believe, built with a workforce varying as needed between 14,000 and 40,000, over ten years. Instruction could be face to face, techniques given by example. Egyptians around 3000 BCE used fired bricks, as did the late Romans, who fabricated with poured concrete during the 3rd century BCE.

Culture is the personality of a people

Culture is the personality of a people, and the artistries are its language, as readers of this essay may consider. The artistries of developing societies reveal the culture most vividly, will give rise to a canon, and will often influence the direction it will take. In many societies the written or sung artistries were to become influential. In ancient Greece it was architecture.

A propensity for, or the possibility of, a splendid, intricate structure, to be thought culturally graceful, grand, even wondrous, did not enter the imagination of the Mediterranean architects until they were made fit to receive it. This by the development of a written form able to provide a canon of work in the culture into which it would grow, a regime to test the competing possibilities within a tradition of learning and apprenticeship.

Hellenic scholar Michael W. Palmer wrote online:

After the collapse of the Mycenaean civilisation around 1200 BCE writing disappeared from Greece. In the late 9th to early 8th century BCE a script based on the Phoenician syllabary was introduced.[14]

This is Hellenic Greek of the classical period, the written language of educated Greeks, including the great philosophers of the age, carrying the texts of Plato's Republic, Thucydides' histories, Democritus' atomic theories of the universe. Since its introduction during 800 BCE, this language used around 200 generations to improve its capacities, carrying knowledge and understanding in many disciplines, to share the consciousness of thinkers from one era to another. A spectacular division of this momentum happened in architecture, building a canon of works, a regime to test the competing possibilities, carrying a heritage of learning. From a tradition throughout Europe of slab, block or rubble structures, Athens now produced the architects Itkinos, Callicrates and Phidias to design a building of grace, splendour, symmetrical poise, which might reference the heavens. It was of an immensity sufficient to please Athena, their patron Goddess.

This is the Parthenon.

---

14 See Michael W. Palmer's website: https://blog.greek-language.com

Five centuries, perhaps twenty-five or so generations later, the Romans began work on the Colosseum to display spectacle theatre.

A character

A character written early in the life of modern theatre, say Sophocles' Antigone, 2500 years ago, would by now have watched the art's beginnings, at first in thrall to religions, then progress to a liberality in which theatre is permitted to turn its attention to humankind. Antigone, in her early performances, was a character reacting to the will of the gods, now becoming more moving to current audiences as a dutiful young daughter acting out a sadness at the human predicament, or in hope of escaping it. A propensity in the artistries towards some sharing of consciousness, through the empathies and the exchange of emotional information, is detectable in several societies, particularly in the now written artistries, if religion doesn't forbid.

To attempt a reconstruction of the origins of theatre, by beginning with a scrutiny of drama in the golden age of European playing, might be justified if only for the excitement in it.

The flowering of Florence, despite its efforts at citizen governance, was due to the influence of powerful families during the early Renaissance. With immortality in mind, the triumphs in artistries were spectacularly in architecture, sculpture and painting but, in the literary arts, less than in the physical. Nevertheless, Leonardo da Vinci published a treatise on painting that affected the entire art world.

Priestly trade in redemption by the sinful wealthy, to ease their paths into heaven after life, was profitable for the princes of the Church but drew the attention of reformers throughout Western Europe: Erasmus, Luther, Calvin, Zwingli. Protestantism provided a variation to established Christianity and would become the selected variation in its birthplaces, then drawing into its circle England at the direction of Henry VIII with Cromwell and Cranmer. The gradual and hesitant expansion of the Reformation movements in Europe permitted the rise of a merchant class alongside growing professional and artisan, at the expense of the old Church and of some princedoms. Churches and nunneries were sold off, trade routes to the East established, and across the Mediterranean wherever they could avoid Muslim pirates. Italy, Portugal and Spain remained loyal to the Vatican and prospered early. Philip II took Spain to European dominance, married Queen Mary of England, after her death beggared Spain's treasuries with the defeat of his holy Armada, died ruling a bankrupt nation, while his enemy Elizabeth enjoyed a kingdom enriched by trade and piracy.

London now began its Golden Age of Theatre. The Reformation enabled theatre to move beyond the religious Mystery Plays into complex humanist drama, the expansion of middle-class wealth enabled patronage and commissioning of theatres. The Renaissance was spreading from Italy to Southern England. Soon Spain, freed of the inhibitions of Philip II, would be surprised by a growing patronage of its theatres, ready for the popularity of Cervantes and others now forgotten. London was readying for Fletcher, Beaumont, Jonson, Middleton, Rowley, Massinger, Marlowe, Shakespeare. For a penny each, paupers crowded the dirt floor of the theatres, for a threepennny coin the wealthier sat at third level with a cushion, to sorrow over the disappointments of jilted Aspatia, to despair with Othello's cry, 'O fool, fool, fool.'

Many primitive religions carry an impediment to human social development, the imperative of the sacred, the invariable. The stultifying effect of sacredness has a Paleolithic history, the origins preserved for us over 50 or 60 millennia by cave painting, notably in northern Australian culture, showing theatrical performances of actors, singers, dancers with headdresses and implements, as in performances seen in first European contact. These paintings and others elsewhere suggest to us theatre's origins were commonly in service of a religion. By the time of Elizabethan Europe, the pace of change in theatre was rapid. Cultural changes first by the Reformation then the Renaissance through Europe were decisive in allowing theatre to develop from pious tableaux, coarse mimicry and biblical intonement to humanist empathies, sharing experience, sharing emotion, sharing a consciousness. This radical progression in content and style of the time is remarkable for the astonishing refinement of language and the use of dramatic poignancies of opportunity and misfortune.

Inheritors of the theatrical traditions in Britain, and of the French tragedians Racine with Corneille followed by the deft Molière, or then later the fillip to German drama in Vienna and Berlin, are readily given pause by one of the frequent modern revivals from ancient Greece, Euripides' *Medea*, which first saw production in 431 BCE. Aristophanes' *Lysistrata* appeared a few years later, one year before Sophocles' *Oedipus Rex*. The gods of the day were tolerant of variations in the ways they might be portrayed, so the priestly caste was not vigilant for possible blasphemies. The claim 'I am a jealous God' had not yet occurred to a deity so, until the establishment of Christianity in Rome, the dramatic muse was permitted to experiment with plot and utterance. Priests were yet to become the dramaturges. Greek tragedies avoided religious banishment for many centuries. *Lysistrata* was banned nearly three millennia later by the USA's Comstock Law in 1873, judged immoral, and *Oedipus Rex* banned during the last days of Queen Victoria's England, a portrayal of incest.

Development of theatre in Africa is thought to be associated with dance and music, many celebrating the myths of creation and in praise of protective deities. As Northern Africa fell under the influence of Islam, gatherings became gender segregated, representation of revered figures was prohibited, and entertainment became despised.

An impediment not too different was to surprise much of North America under Christianity nearly a thousand years later. From 1750 CE onward, most US states banned play performance. Timothy Dwight IV, president in 1794 of the ecclesiastical Yale College, warned of playgoing as a sinful indulgence causing loss of one's immortal soul. American theatre was rescued from Puritan dogma by pride in the success of the Revolution, as producers warmed to the popular themes of battlefield valor and sacrifice.

Theatre made its gift to the influence of audience connection when the Athenian actor Thespis was permitted to step forward from the ranks of the Greek Chorus to play a unique character, with mask and gesture. Thus making possible a dramatic focus on individual emotion, reaction to fortune, plight, threat, relief, joy, affection. We have no evidence of a similar development elsewhere. Asia and the Middle East were in thrall to puppetry, solid or in shadows, Africa to song and dance. The Americas of the era are hidden.

Again the societies of Australia are useful, as the world's oldest existing cultures. Here the players were presenting events of Dreamtime and Creation, where the characters were forces, often in animal form, rather than individuals. When Thespis made his step forward, here was a permitted variation which, as in biology, would be selected or perish according to its fitness for the circumstances through which it may make its way. Much would be written about character acting, the Semiotics of Acting and the transfer of emotion from player to audience. So well would this method of consciousness sharing select for theatrical longevity as to be able to carry its momentum through the mediums yet to be invented, proscenium, film, radio, television.

Facemasks claim a degree of universality that is remarkable, but few were to do with a representation of human emotion, a transfer of feeling, a sharing of consciousness. In theatre, because a mask's expression is fixed, one cannot command an emotional range, except for those like the clever Japanese *kumadori*, which alter expression according to the angle at which they are tilted. Otherwise, the most common expression is ferocity. Early masks used, say, for Medea, who murdered her children to spite her deserting husband Jason, were stylised, and gave way to face-paint for the task. By the time Medea had made a way over 2500 years to modern Europe, Angelique Rockas played her without make-up, allowing a teardrop to roll down a bare cheek on its heartbreaking journey, taking Medea through shock, sorrow, fury.

Fine character performances

Fine character performances, transmitting emotional information, call in comparisons with the development of portrait painting. Ancient portraiture, if any existed, is yet lost to us, but the solids persist. We have figures and faces in carvings and clay made 20,000 years ago in Central Europe, Japan and then Iraq, much from Egypt and the Pharaohs. Representations of rulers are efforts in praise and fealty, but portraiture is at its most useful to the development of civilisations where it exhibits human reaction and character. Aristotle's most quoted dictum is: 'The aim of art is to represent not the outward significance of things but their inward significance.' Not until the stone head of an Attic youth described as 'a pupil of Rampin Master' from about 560 BCE Athens do we find a work of character. Here, a smile of good nature and irreverent nonchalance, familiar in youth today.

Not far away in time, but a vast distance south east, the Cham people of the Southern Mekong region were sculpting figures and busts in sandstone, using techniques of volume and surfacing as sophisticated as the Greeks. Scowls and grimaces familiar to humankind were adapted to the fierce animal gods of their Hindu ancestors.

Painting became an expert fiction but is unlikely to have begun this way, since worldwide through prehistory the arts seem to have begun as a religious duty, with no exceptions we know about. Such is the dominance of fear as a human emotion, with the need for supernatural protection. The early works were event paintings populated with mythological figures in action.

In the case of China, and its later borrower Japan, the influence was to become Buddhism. In line with the emerging virtues of restraint and renunciation, the drawn figures were graceful in line, facial features sparse and abbreviated. Sub-Saharan figurative art in Africa remained dominated by carving and rock paintings of animal and human figures.

Pre-Islamic Arab artists used sculpture and relief enhanced with paint for animals and human figures, in styles suggesting they were familiar with Hellenic technique flowing east into the Levant. The spread of Islam halted artistry in the sculpture of human form in case the object might incite worship. Their artists turned to enhancing the magnificence of mosques and tributes to the Almighty, later raising the decoration we now call Arabesque. Jews were also sensitive to the sinfulness of worshipping graven images, so little is to be found of the figurative in their panels and floor tiles of the time.

In the Mediterranean, the Greco Roman gods were not precious about their ascribed appearance, although they were known to play cruel jests with the fates of their subjects when displeased. Sculptors vied for praise when producing busts of Zeus, Apollo, Athena, Aphrodite, each a variation on a previous vision.

The Egyptian era had produced stonework busts of Pharaohs to enrich their afterlife, so visages were moulded with respect and character was wisely absent. Works of sculptors in less pious Rome began to outshine the religious Egyptians by about 350 BCE. Busts by Lysippos of Alexander the Great show finer dimensional modelling than anyone before. Improvement continued through late Rome, busts of Julius Caesar, Brutus, Mark Anthony, Octavian, and Tiberius who ruled Rome and its territories when Jesus was a young man.

From this period survive multiple busts of individual nobles, two of Titus, four of Trajan, three of Hadrian, several of Nero, of the inquisitive Hippocrates, features now so telling we grasp likenesses. Never mind these are the visions of individual sculptors, these ancient celebrities have become people we would recognise face to face. We would know Herodotus if we saw him in the street.

And, magically now, the first appearance of painted portraits

And, magically now, the first appearance of painted portraits, surviving because they are on stone tablets. From some year between 20 and 30 CE/AD a colour-painted marble panel 'A Woman and a Man', possibly Semitic subjects, from Pompeii. From ca 60 CE/AD a marvellous coloured fresco also from Pompeii, 'A Studious Girl'. Here she is, auburn haired, holding a tablet, the end of her stylus wet between pursed lips, now taken by an idea, eyes in space gaze, thinking deeply, a true portrait, holding open forever a brief moment. Watching this we know we are present at a transition to a new medium capable of transmitting personal consciousness, an artistry which can be executed more swiftly than sculpting, and by an artist alone.

Around the 330s Constantine converted to Christianity and brought the empire with him. As with the populace, artists were slow to change their culture, which required the passing of four or five generations, so the humanistic tradition persisted awhile. By the 550s, paintings of religious events, ritual paintings, had become the artistic focus.

In frescoes of Bishop Maximian in San Vitale, 'Christ Treading the Beasts' at Ravenna, Evangelist Mark in Rossano, and the Virgin and Child at Sinai in which the babe resembles an ill-tempered adult, these faces had lost any fine modelling. Figures were stiffly posed, the golden halo was making its appearance, artistry had again become event narratives, scriptural, subservient, variations not to be permitted, so improvement, as Darwin and Wallace and Chambers would later explain to us, was not possible.

Religion again demanded obedience from artistry. Sacredness, the iron chastity belt, was locked into place.

We might be content with this symmetry of artistic progression had not a small band of well diggers in a field near Xi'an in Central China, during March 1974, found they were bringing to the surface fragments of terracotta statues of warriors. These proved to be an army 8000 or so strong, interred under twenty hectares of grassland. After decades of reconstruction by archeologists the army is now described as the afterlife guardians of emperor Qin Shi Huang's mausoleum. Each warrior with individual facial expression, imperious, kindly, distrustful, surprised, and others. The artisans of the time were skilled in depicting character and emotion, abilities later lost.

Under permissive Buddhism

Under permissive Buddhism, artists in China and Japan were improving the skill of the likeness and experimenting with dimension and perspective. From the early 1200s several pieces survive of the Japanese sculptor in wood, Unkei. His form of the priest Muchaku in Kofuku-ji temple in Nara, shows a face in which we may see wisdom and age, at the same time a childlike trust, reflecting the Buddhist association of childishness and purity.

Unkei's statue of the logician Vasubandhu catches him delivering rhetoric, hands in mid gesture. Unkei is thought to have been experimenting with distortions of human proportions to create illusions of movement.

From around 1239, we have a painting of the monk Wuzun Shifan, held now in Kyoto but attributed to an unknown Chinese painter, showing the seated monk holding a rolled scroll, inquisitive of eye, perhaps about to speak, calm, sage. The background is skin colour, so the face is given substance only by the skillful inkwork of the head and face.

All these works are intelligent and beautiful, all figures to which we are drawn to make a judgement of human character. The slump in portraitist performance in Christian Europe persisted until the early 1400s. Three Flemish masters and members of the Guild of Painters were admired in Belgium, given sensational standing in the late 1400s throughout Europe: van Eyck, Campin and van der Weylen.

Robert Campin, quickly to be known as the Master of Flemalle, was working on the first developments in oil-based paints, far brighter than egg tempera. Paintings of dress fabrics were now given bulk and sheen. His portrait of Saint Veronica follows tradition, she displays her veil which had cleaned Jesus' face and now bears his likeness. Her expression expects the viewer's reaction, shock. All others of the dozens of paintings attempting this scene fail to engage the subject with the viewer as does this work of 1410.

Donors of Mechelen shows a husband and wife walking from a doorway, perhaps of a church, a beggar behind them, the door ajar enough to show buildings of the city around a town square. The far perspective securely grounds the closer scene in the further world. On the right-side panel of the Werl Altarpiece, Campin arranges the young Saint Barbara seated before a hearth reading the Holy Book by firelight in a library, high ceiling beams and symmetrical lintels, a view of parkland beyond its window. This perfect perspective gives the mythological girl a solid dimension in the real world.

Campin's pupil Rogier van der Weyden would outshine him. Of Rogier's portraits, three ladies of rank are magnificent. The first, now known as *The Wimple*, shows a woman wearing a white headdress, her gaze alert and inquisitive, as if wary of the interest the viewer is showing in her. The head of *Isabella of Portugal*, a faint smile, wearing a rich brocade painted to give it weight and bulk, a bouffant veil, the translucent brim rests on her brow like a whisper. In *Portrait of a Lady* her downcast gaze is contemplative, serene, a presence confident of attention, again the veil, its brim as transparent as a delicate fabric yet to be invented. To show the sweep of his skill we might well choose *Seven Sacraments Alterpiece*, Jesus on a lofty cross over the nave, the crowd below in multiple portraiture, around them stone columns soar, arches meet at a zenith above; this is a splendid architectural space, vast and reverberant, the repetition of the many cornices a metaphor for a ceaseless echo.

Masters from the Low Countries, van Eyck, Campin, van der Weyden, soon to be joined by Rembrandt and Vermeer, were making European sensibilities fit to receive great painters from Italy, Germany, France, enabling masterliness in Durer, Raphael, Leonardo da Vinci, Titian, the Holbeins, Michelangelo. Artistries here were delivering a message to the established religions: mere piety is not sufficient; the artist, and therefore the viewer, is capable of judgements, of understanding, of some consciousness in common, one with another.

The sudden appearance in Japan of figures

The sudden appearance in Japan of figures displaying emotion is attributed to the master Hokusai. Poet Ota Nanpo was pleased to write in 1818, 'Hokusai skillfully draws any shape, drawing what you can see with your eyes, and what you feel in your heart.'

Portraiture in China remained with the traditional until the 18th century CE, when a small number of Christian missionaries introduced their converts to Western oil techniques, but the subjects were biblical. After 1947 Chinese figure painting chose the scene of the group, since the individual was not important. The temper of heroic struggle, in parallel with the post-revolutionary Soviet Union, and a similarity here in stultification as with the religious sacred became plain, prohibiting the emergence of any variation that might succeed. During the 1980s modern portraits began to appear in Chinese galleries, making use of techniques conveying character and emotional stimulus.

With portraiture in Western Europe, spectacularly the works by Lucien Freud and Francis Bacon, came so deep a sharing of consciousness in the cruelties of the human condition as to cause the viewer near unbearable pain.

The reach of song to share emotions

The reach of song to share emotions may seem the more poignant if a spectacular example is taken first.

The most affecting song in all Western opera may be 'One Fine Day', from Puccini's 1904 *Madama Butterfly*, in which Cio-Cio-san sings of her love for absent American husband Pinkerton. During 1997 the New Zealand soprano Dame Kiri Te Kanawa performed the aria in remote South Australian Flinders Ranges, the escarpment of Yalkarinha Gorge as her proscenium. She sang of Butterfly's love for her absconded husband, whom we all know has divorced her and taken an American bride, and of the joy she will feel on that fine day when she watches from the hill as his ship enters the harbour, bringing him faithfully back to her. A silence fell on the final notes of that performance, lasting long enough that some observers feared the audience might be so emotionally in thrall as to lose the capacity for applause.

Ancient song most likely was in service to religion: Songs in Praise. From Sumer about 2000 years BCE, we have a hymn to Lipit-Ishtar, a god–king noted for his proclamation of a Code of Law.

> The adornment of royal power am I,
> Lipit-Ishtar, the son of the god Enlil, am I,
> The one who lifts the highest shepherd's staff, the life of the land of Sumer, am I,
> The farmer who pours forth his piles of grain, am I,
> The shepherd who increases the male and female fatlings in the sheep-pen, am I,
> The one who lets fish and birds flourish in the swamps, am I,
> The one who brings ever-flowing water in abundance to the watercourses, am I,
> The one who increases the luxuriant yields of the great mountains, am I.

The temper of the song is fealty, and respect for the grandeur of the god–king leaves no space for the emotional content of the singer beyond piety.

In Mesoamerica, Peter Watson notes in his book *Ideas*: 'there was hardly any instrumental music anywhere on the continent because, in the normal course of events, song, dance and music went together in ritual'.[15]

---

15 Peter Watson, *Ideas: A History of Thought and Invention, from Fire to Freud*, Harper Perennial, 2006.

Pre-Islamic Arab song traditions extended to the enslavement of songstresses, whose repertoire seems restricted to fealty to their wealthy owners and to high-ranked warriors. The demands of piety fettered song, as it fettered all artistic forms, with no exceptions, anywhere. As Islamic influence expanded through the Middle East and Asia only Songs in Praise were permitted, and the use of music for pleasure became censored, although less strictly in those Muslim countries with strong folk music traditions, such as in Indonesian instrumentalism. As these words are written, reports appear in the international press from Pakistan of widespread assassination of singers and other musicians who practise secular music, who are regarded as sinners.

The Mesopotamian Psalms, including King David's, were chants or Songs in Praise. Otherwise, laments, supplications or codes of lore.

Song to share human emotion, rather than simply fealty, appears earlier than one might have expected. 'Song of Songs', attributed to Solomon, son of David, who ruled Israel/Judah about the 10th century BCE, at first sight appears as an erotic love piece.

> Let him kiss me with the kisses of his mouth,
> For your love is better than wine;
> your anointing oils are fragrant …
> While the king was on his couch
> my nard gave forth its fragrance.

> My beloved is to me a sachet of myrrh that lies between my breasts.

Its interest is that in a study of human development, its artistry is not crushed by piety. The content is not pious, the lovers praise only each other, the pleasure they take in their lovemaking is their subject. Clearly it reaches us from an impious era. Following a period in which song was fettered by religious fealty, the political structure had relaxed sufficiently to allow the appearance of a variation, the emergence of emotional transfer in song, a sharing of consciousness, the singer affecting the listeners emotionally.

The variation was then available to natural selection, but religion was successful in delaying it. Judaism moved to reinterpret the song as metaphorically presenting God's love for Israel, rather than an eroticism. During the 2nd century CE, Rabbi Akiba held that anyone treating the 'Song of Songs' otherwise, 'as if it were a vulgar song forfeits his share in the world to come'. Christianity saw the attraction of this legal fiction, accepting the redefinition, substituting God's love for Israel with God's love for the Church. Solomon is recognised as a major prophet in Islam, without attributing the song to him.

Dance began

Dance began, the assumption runs, for devotion, for supplication, and became useful for recording sacred rites and passing on histories and legends before the advent of writing. In northern Australia, the oldest living cultures, dance movements spoke of creation forces often personified by mythical animals. Chinese dancers, not bound by strictures of sacredness therefore permitting variations that might become popular, performed shamanist ritual. They progressed as entertainers at courtly functions, sometimes on show in their hundreds and, as today, their gymnastic content was generally high. Since their tradition is of costume and mask, audience emotional response is restricted to admiration. Ballet is of recent development. Beginning in the Florentine reign of the Medici, it was perhaps too young to have much influenced the sharing of emotional values in our societies.

Emotional transfer from performer to audience was a movement given impetus during the Romantic era. It would seem a creature of recent centuries were it not for the spectacular exception of India. Somewhere close to the beginning of time, Brahma directed the sage Bharata to codify technique in the performed arts of

India, in the form of an epic poem, the *Natyashastra*, possibly dating from 220 BCE, still the template for excellence today. It applauds performers who affect the audience with *rasa*, emotion.

Rhythm, repetition and attractive conjunctions of sounds

Rhythm, repetition and attractive conjunctions of sounds give poesy memorability, fair evidence for its development throughout humankind before we were able to preserve important thought in enduring form, writing.

The Tale of the Shipwrecked Sailor in Egyptian Hieratic, dates from around 2500 BCE, and follows the travails of the castaway as a dramatic history, and Gabriel Garcia Marquez's version retains the impersonal tone. *The Epic of Gilgamesh* followed from Sumer maybe 500 years later, a mythical history of Uruk. Both epics, as with the *Odyssey* and the Sanskrit *Ramayana* and *Mahabharata*, are too long for recitation true to their written form, so likely were extended during the early literate age.

The magnificent tradition of classical Chinese poetry was encouraged by many successive emperors, each ruler establishing a new formal style. With the collapse of the Ming Dynasty during the 1600s CE, content became more emotionally charged and socially responsive. Poetry working as an agent of emotional transfer, as in empathy, more closely approaching the tradition of Japanese Haiku which, from the mid 1400s CE, dealt in the currency of exquisite sensibility.

> First autumn morning
> the mirror I stare into
> shows my father's face.
>
> Murakami Kijo
> Born Tokyo, 1865

The bondage of piety loosened in Europe with the Renaissance, for poetry as for theatre, allowing variations instead of forbidding them, so available for selection. Again this enabled Shakespeare, in poetry as in theatre, although separating the poetic from the theatrical here is unrewarding. The first lines of Romeo and Juliet meeting each other, running the lines together, makes a sonnet.

> ROMEO [To JULIET]
> If I profane with my unworthiest hand
> This holy shrine, the gentle fine is this:

> My lips, two blushing pilgrims, ready stand
> To smooth that rough touch with a tender kiss.
>
> JULIET
> Good pilgrim, you do wrong your hand too much,
> Which mannerly devotion shows in this;
> For saints have hands that pilgrims' hands do touch,
> And palm to palm is holy palmers' kiss.
>
> ROMEO
> Have not saints lips, and holy palmers too?
>
> JULIET
> Ay, pilgrim, lips that they must use in prayer

Dean of St Paul's, in 1621, was an influence in leading poetry away from the solely pious to the humanitarian. This was John Donne. Famously:

> Any man's death diminishes me
> because I am involved in mankind
> and therefore never send to know
> for whom the bell tolls,
> it tolls for thee.

And the poesies of love:

> And now good-morrow to our waking souls,
> Which watch not one another out of fear;
> For love all love of other sights controls,
> And makes one little room an everywhere.

Since the iron grip of religions were relaxed, poetry had moved into realms of emotion transfer, poet to reader, fine adjustments of sensibilities.

> The form of the poem, in other words, is crucial to poetry's power to do the thing which always is and always will be to poetry's credit: the power to persuade that vulnerable part of *our consciousness* of its rightness in spite of the evidence of wrongness all around it...
>
> Seamus Heaney, *Open Ground: Selected poems, 1966–1996*

Music is the purest fiction now

Music is the purest fiction now, although it likely began everywhere as reproduction of sounds gathered from the natural world: birdsong, animal cries, wind and water, echoes. In northern Australia the leap of a kangaroo persists in musical rhythms. The mechanisms by which music in the West persuades emotional response in Europeans excites argument in psychologists and musicologists.

Western music moved through phases of the devotional and the courtly roles of heraldry and dance, later coming to a form, sometimes called a narrative in which competing developments finally come to a resolution, come to a satisfaction with each other, producing emotional sensibility. This poignancy in response is most often attributed to Beethoven; the music of all prior composers led to Beethoven, all later composers draw from him.

The influence in China of music was proscribed during the age of the philosopher Mozi around 400 BCE, since he considered it an indulgence and not useful to his passion 'universal love' and cultural harmony. Two millennia later, the Cultural Revolution under Mao discouraged music that produced any emotion other than pride in the revolutionary movement. Outside these aberrations Chinese music from the time of the Yellow Emperor, 4500 years ago, avoided the barrier of sacredness that the Abrahamic religions imposed on much of the West. It was encouraged to engage the emotions of listeners as a prime function, supported by each of the great dynasties.

> If the audience is not moved by the music, particularly if it is a masterpiece from the *guqin* core repertoire, it is usually the player's fault and not the listener's.[16]
>
> Professor Li Xiangting, *guqin* master

The artistries most discrete and peculiar to their cultures are cuisine and music. Foodstuffs are in common: the proteins, vegetation, grains are everywhere prominent, oils and lactations. Most cultures are drawn to sugars and salt, as are other animals and insects. In the arrangement of tastes a culture shows its strength,

---

16 Professor Li Xiangting, Guqin lecture at the Center of Chinese Studies, University of California, Berkeley, 3 December 2009.

so Asian cooking techniques were considered stridently alien to European and African palates.

Prehistory, conquests and invasions must have increased the range of edibles in all cultures, as in recorded times. Perhaps 400 generations of chefs in Chinese regional cuisines have cooked with herbs and spices traded along the Silk Road to the Mediterranean beginning in the Han dynasty. Cuisines in Asia and Europe then expanded with the arrival of new vegetable strains from the New World. Asian cuisines were slow to penetrate Europe, but in California and Australia the gold rushes of the mid 1800s drew Chinese people, largely from Guangdong, establishing Cantonese cuisine there earlier than in the rest of the world.

Music approaches cuisine in its splendid isolation, culture from culture, but not everywhere. Western European cultures became homogenous. African music, because of its association with dance, was rapidly understood by European invaders and, as a byproduct of the practice of slavery through the Americas, its rhythms became the driving components in jazz. Westerners have generally felt music, and opera, from the Chinese cultures impenetrable, but the reverse does not hold true. At the time of writing, Chinese practitioners are affected by an admiration for Western instrumentalism. So we currently see an institution follow the order of change: variation, to inheritance or passing on, to popular selection; very nearly as if it were following the biological pattern.

Dealing with the development of artistries invites argument about the concept of beauty, a crowded and noisy forum. Religious explanations abound. Immanuel Kant in the late 1700s influenced German philosophy, then all of Western culture, describing a recognition of beauty as possible only when it allows 'the free play' of the mind 'independent of interest'. More culturally determined explanations of beauty followed and long held sway with the rise of sociology. Only to be rejected by philosopher Professor Denis Dutton in 2010 with his TED Talk *A Darwinian Theory of Beauty*, in admiration of prehistoric stone tools 'the earliest known works of art'.

So the next time you pass a jewelry shop window displaying a beautifully cut teardrop-shaped stone, don't be so sure it's just your culture telling you that that sparkling jewel is beautiful. Your distant ancestors loved that shape and found beauty in the skill needed to make it ...

This theory is linear historical, rather than Darwinian, it does not bear ready extension into music, but it does give weight to 'the rich emotional lives of our most ancient ancestors' and 'to the expression of emotion in art'. Does it suggest a path to a description of beauty beginning with a striking natural event or presence that may then be abstracted, refined, purified by artistic effort, enhancing its message?

The function of the artistries

The function of the artistries is to be expressive. They have developed far beyond their ritual origins, retarded only in those cultures that hold fast to religious tenets of inviolable sacredness. The momentum of artistries now, toward emotional transfer and so toward a more generally shared consciousness is a force, an impulse, worthy of account. If an artistry and its culture develop beyond the authority of the ruling class, the emperors, tsars, shahs, chieftains, on to a popular domain, and are allowed variation, do they then select for properties of affinity, of emotional transfer, some consciousness in common? The evidence of artistries we have examined here suggests this.

If the momentum of the artistries, as the language of their culture, favours human affinity and a consciousness in common, they face countervailing forces. Religion fights in the front line, invariably the less developed versions. Where a religion takes account of rational enquiry and modifies to match the realities it finds in the world, as did Islam in the Abbasid Golden Age, as did Classical Greece, as did Anglicanism around Darwin, as do Muhammadiyah and Nahdlatul Ulama in Indonesia, its resistance lacks ferocity and modifies readily. Where a religion remains primitive, because dogma prohibits rational enquiry into the working of the world, resistance to any movement of affinity, any approach to a commonality of consciousness, can be murderous, genocidal.

We have seen this play out in Christian Europe, the Americas, the Middle East, and now again with the Islamic State movement. Currently the USA shows how mistaken one may be in confusing a nation with a culture. Few nations now are of the one culture, sharing a social personality, particularly in the modern Western hemisphere. The USA, Great Britain, Australia, much of modern Europe, all share conflicting cultures. Social persuasions have divided those who admire cooperative societies from those preferring an arena of rivalries, of competing antagonists, both groups placing a separate value upon social cohesion, the dominion selection.

Religions spectacularly defend against variations with fortifications of sacredness prohibiting tolerance as apostasy. A technique copied by some secular political creeds, in Albania, in China, in Pol Pot's Kampuchea, and in the USSR where Stalin selected the Catalan Communist Youth's Ramon Mercader to assassinate Trotsky in Mexico, then honouring the lad as a hero of the Soviet Union.

The Cultural Revolution in China illuminated the Gang of Four as worshippers of the sacredness of its ideology as if a liturgy. Applauding Zhou Enlai as the Father of Modern China is politically polite currently.

Whether Zhou or successors Hua Guofeng or Deng Xiaoping were one more than another responsible for modern China, clearly they all allowed a choice for reform. This provided the variation that a living institution relies upon for the possibility of improvement and therefore survival, so the needs of imaginary arrangements follow biology. Vietnam, soon after victory in the American War, adopted a pluralist philosophy and, from the year 2000, became one of the world's fastest growing economies. Laos lags behind but is also taking a pluralist path.

Parliamentary states have achieved intransigence by use of the charge Treason, or with a rigid constitution. The USA's bulwark against change is seen in its defence of its primitive constitution with zealotry to be compared with the religious.

In fear of a predatory world

In fear of a predatory world and in need to answer the three questions, 'How to survive?', 'How to successfully forage?' and 'How to avoid predators?', humankind, seemingly universally, was encouraged to hold religions dear, for over 10,000 generations from our beginning as *Homo sapiens,* before an alternative appeared. We held to beliefs of almost infinite varieties, said to be decrees issued by our creators, obedient to them throughout the world, on available records, until the rise of the Ionian culture on the east coast of the Aegean Sea six centuries BCE. In this centre stood the city Miletus.

> In this city the power was in the hands of the merchants, and the priesthood had no significant social impact, Ionian intellectuals were nor heavily influenced by religion, nor

limited by ancient books claiming truth or divine revelation.[17]

Here lived a mathematician and astronomer Thales, who presented his intellectual circle with a resource to rival the scriptures in understanding the world and its works.

This was enquiry.

With his students Anaxamander and Anaximones, Thales formed the Milesian School, strengthening secular enquiry into the world and its origin. These were the first evolutionists. In moving towards an understanding of naturally guided causes and effects, away from divine arrangement, they were keeping pace with the increasing knowledge of the structure of the human body by physicians. Domestic medical practitioners still regarded recovery from illness as a gift from the gods, but military practitioners were moving towards a secular understanding. As we have seen in our current lifetimes, medical advances are rapid in times of war. In European hospitals during its two great conflicts, in Belfast hospitals' skill in reattaching severed limbs during their Troubles, so medicos in the Ionian wars attending injuries knew amputation, and the effects of blood loss, bone and brain damage. Soon Almaeon, a pupil of Pythagoras,

---

17 Quoted in Cristian Violatti, 'Ionia and the Ionian Revolt (499–494 BCE)', 27 May 2014, https://notesinhistory.blogspot.com

would begin dissections to record anatomical forms, and Hippocrates advance the study of clinical medicine.

Nothing of Thales' work survives, only fragments from Anaxamander and Anaximones. We rely on their histories from Aristotle, Herodotus and Diogenes Laertius. Original papers of the period were burned over the succeeding millennium with the destruction of the great libraries in Alexandria, Antioc, Cordoba and western Persia. Seen as storehouses of heresies, they were destroyed on orders from popes and caliphs with the spread of Christianity and Islam, as efforts to prevent variation, including improvement.

The Greeks in their Classical era

The Greeks in their Classical era took to enquiry and to the search for knowledge with enthusiasm then unmatched anywhere in the world. Prominent in examination of methods designed to best service the gathering of information, and testing claims to the status of knowledge, beginning epistemology, was Plato. He began a tireless, even laborious, pursuit of authenticity, the practice of poetry as his early target, in search of deviance, the poet's fraud, representing the subject as it appears to be, not as in reality.

His argument was elaborate. To conjure a plain example of fraudulence, his choice is a piece of furniture, in this case a bed. This bed has three originators: God, who created the idea, the possibility of a bed; a craftsman who creates this very bed; and an artist, a painter, who creates merely a representation of this very bed. The god and the craftsman are creators of this very bed, the painter creates merely a reference to the bed, which is untrue, a chimera, therefore the painter is a charlatan, as is a poet.

The critique was written into his *Republic* and makes more than one appearance. His argument itself makes use of a dramatic contrivance: Plato's executed mentor is resurrected and the argument is presented to the reader as if the record of a conversation between Socrates, in his lifetime, and a colleague Glaucon. Socrates is drawn as a philosophical seer of impeccable rationality, Glaucon as an intellectual companion, respectful, at times shy.

Here Plato is the dramatist, presenting a fiction as if history, himself the artist creating an appearance, as do the poets and painters he despised. An indulgence, perhaps, he chose to leave brazen to perplex Platonic scholars for millennia.

An acquired urge

An acquired urge in humankind to share knowledge likely led to the early use of mimetics. Some anthropologists suggest first use of this, or of language, was religious. No, more likely early gestures were of warning rather than devotion, 'Look behind you' rather than 'Gods are great'.

If we accept Merlin Donald's timing for mimetics, beginning with *Homo erectus*, and Peter Watson's belief that language was under development by *Homo habilis* because of their hunting, group and kin patterns, anatomically modern humans appeared during eras of language development. This emerged as an effective system around 200,000 years ago, or perhaps 10,000 generations after the appearance of mimetics. Another thousand generations saw attempts at writing.

Momentum for knowledge gathering, storage and transmission was growing. We can plot approximate eras for appearances of song, poetry, writing, libraries, printing, communication codes with smoke, flags, semaphore, Morse, then telegraph, radio, radar, telephone, television, the internet. The number of human generations between each stage was lessening. The generations necessary after the development of writing to progress into printing was about 200. For advances from Marconi's 1895 discovery of 'wireless' transmission to television transmission required one generation.

Construction of the first electronic computers in the late 1950s, until the World Wide Web required one half the life of physicist Tim Berners-Lee, providing the stupendous shared consciousness now available to us. Its inventor refused patent or ownership. During its celebrations at the 2012 Summer Olympics in London, his message shone in coloured lights: *This is For Everyone*, it read.

No need of gods

'No need of gods' was the thesis of Thales of Miletus, the mysteries of existence we are able to solve by reason. For the first time in the history of the world, some part of humankind could turn away from a search for divine instruction towards a learning by empirical experience. Two and a half millennia on, we are watching the volume of that learning soar with astonishing acceleration in the recording, storage and transmission of information.

Hal B. Becker in 1986 asserted:

> the recording density achieved by Gutenberg was approximately 500 characters per square inch – 500 times the density of (4000 BCE) Sumerian clay tablets. By the year 2000, semiconductor random access memory should be storing 1.25×10^{11} bytes per cubic inch.[18]

---

18 Hal B. Becker, 'Can users really absorb data at today's rates? Tomorrow's?', *Data Communications*, July 1986.

So the expression of volume now moved from exponents to invent new units of digital volume, the petabytes and exabytes, by the year 2000.

Bounie and Gille, during 2012 in the USA, estimated the world produced 14.7 exabytes of new information in 2008, nearly triple the volume of information in 2003.[19] Most of this will never be subject to human enquiry, it will be trawled by search engines programmed to find topics and keywords. The proportion of religious learning in the total of retained data seems tiny. The Pew Research Centre estimates world population with no religion as about 15 per cent of our 7.4 billion.[20] In an attempt to estimate a volume of current religious scholarship, one may search the Web, which will disclose that the Society of Biblical Literature claims membership by 8000 living scholars, vastly outrunning those religious competitors in which scholarship is restricted by a governing hierarchy: twenty-eight scholars are listed in Hindu studies, seventy-one Jewish Biblical scholars, 156 scholars in Islam. Clearly secular scholarship in disciplines from astrophysics to zoology, make up the bulk of exabytes now.

---

19 D. Bounie and L. Gille, 'International Production and Dissemination of Information', *International Journal of Communication*, volume 6, 2012.

20 Pew Research Centre, 'The Global Religious Landscape', 18 December 2012, www.pewresearch.org/religion

Repeating the same mistake

Repeating the same mistake while hoping for a different result is the definition of insanity, so runs a maxim attributed to Albert Einstein or Mark Twain, both without evidence. 'Sanity' came to English from Latin *sanitas*, health. 'Insanity', as a term of art, became too vague of meaning to be of use in medicine. The list of recognised mental aberrations expanded but remained in law, where it was rigorously and narrowly defined. It is now increasingly replaced by 'incompetency', as in the permitted jury verdict, 'Not guilty on the grounds of incompetence.'

Those religions that allow worldly enquiry, empirical knowledge gathering, application of reason, and allow variation enough to accommodate the conclusions, may be seen to become mature. Those that hold to the sacredness of their ancient scriptures, against the weight of growing evidence, to enforce intransigence, remain primitive, so condemning themselves to repeating the same mistakes. The rise of the term 'incompetence' protects us from peril in citing religion as evidence of insanity. Clearly, holding to the sacred, instead of treating with reality as we come to find it, is incompetency.

Post Charles Darwin and his allies, the term 'algorithm' is useful in a broad form: an order of rules of the natural world arranged so compliance with them produces the same result, always. The natural world obeys its algorithms, which we must learn.

Contagious life

Contagious life speeds the birthrate of humankind to 4.3 per seconds now, incubates viruses never before seen, innovates astounding forms like the fungus endemic to the inner surface of jet aircraft fuel tanks, which digest hydrocarbons for sustenance. Richard Dawkins notes a species of worm endemic to German beer mats. Whatever is the formula for all primary algorithms permitting the possibility of life, a convenient term is 'propensity'. Once the minimum requirement in one of the propensities is fulfilled, competition for selection will begin. Any living system that does not provide for variation should lose the struggle and die out.

Are life and consciousness separate phenomena or, as with space time, aspects of the one? The brutality of selection makes the question unimportant. Whatever is the spark of life, a living form without any sentience of its circumstances, or an ability to adjust best to them will die away and, if this ever qualified as a propensity, its demise in the first era of the living must have been swift.

New York sociologist Richard Sennett approves his tutor Hannah Arendt's admiration of the virtues of variation for institutions in his book *The Craftsman*:

Arendt believed that a polity differs from a landmarked building or 'world heritage site': laws should be unstable. The liberal tradition imagines that the rules issuing from deliberation are cast in doubt as conditions change and people ponder further; new provisional rules then come into being.[21]

---

21 Richard Sennett, *The Craftsman*, Penguin Books, 2009.

The soul and consciousness

The soul and consciousness are similar mysteries in parts of secular enquiry.

Peter Watson and Richard Dawkins oppose many of the modern theorists studying consciousness: John Searle at California putting the view that consciousness is an 'emergent property' from the association of neurons; Roger Penrose at London believing it results from activities of quantum physics on nerve cells in the brain; Daniel Dennett at Tufts Boston favouring activities inside the cortex. All these deal with the mechanisms of higher consciousnesses, still influenced by the ancient hunt for the soul, perhaps.

More helpful, for an interest in an initial ignition of consciousness, is enquiry, which allows for the sensing of circumstances and best adjustment to them, observable in life forms without discrete brains. Peter Godfrey-Smith of Sydney and UNY, with an interest in marine life, treats consciousness by selecting a component – cognition – in his *Environmental Complexity Thesis*, so: 'The function of cognition is to enable the agent to deal with environmental complexity.'[22]

David Chalmers at ANU and New York sees consciousness as 'the hardest problem in science and philosophy'. He is dissatisfied with the brain-based analyses, not because he recognises a consciousness in simple reactive life forms like plants and worms, but because they 'do not solve the problem'. Subjective experience, consciousness, is an anomaly, so may require 'a radical idea' to account for it.[23]

The radical idea Chalmers asks us to consider is consciousness as 'one of the fundamental building blocks of the universe'. It exists fundamentally as do, for example, the forces. So consciousness is a prime, as is mass, or gravity, or space/time, or electromagnetism. This interconnectedness of everything, which makes possible our existence was called, in the Mediterranean Classical era, Panpsychism, and is making an appearance again. The Information Explosion may suggest another prime component, the Urge to Knowledge, in partnership with a maxim: Knowledge makes for advantage.

---

22 Peter Godfrey-Smith, 'Environmental Complexity and the Evolution of Cognition', in R. Sternberg and J. Kaufman (eds), *The Evolution of Intelligence*, Lawrence Erlbaum Associates, 2001.

23 David J. Chalmers, *The Conscious Mind: In Search of a Fundamental Theory*, Oxford University Press, 1996.

Here is an echo of beliefs held by Nobel physicist Erwin Schrodinger, who said in 1931:

> Although I think that life may be the result of an accident, I do not think of this consciousness. Consciousness cannot be accounted for in physical terms. For consciousness is absolutely fundamental.[24]

---

24 English translation in R. Chetrite, P. Muratore-Ginanneschi, K. Schwieger, 'E. Schrödinger's 1931 paper "On the Reversal of the Laws of Nature"', The *European Physical Journal H.*, volume 46, number 28, 2021.

Hard problems abound

Hard problems abound. Richard Dawkins in *The Selfish Gene* exhibits a favourite:

> The evolution of the capacity to simulate seems to have culminated in subjective consciousness. Why this should have happened is, to me, the most profound mystery facing modern biology ... Perhaps consciousness arises when the brain's simulation of the world becomes so complete that it must include a model of itself.[25]

He was writing in the context of artificial intelligence and consciousness, from which some part may be borrowed for work on the transmission of emotional information and empathies. May our individual consciousness' 'model of itself' provide the

---

[25] Richard Dawkins, *The Selfish Gene*, Oxford University Press, 1976.

mechanism enabling transmission of emotion? When one becomes aware of another's happy fortune, or unhappy plight, perhaps one's model of oneself provides an intensity of response, joy or sadness, to mirror the other's. We observe that these sympathetic responses are not fated; certain strong institutions may block them. For example, religion may replace one's model with its own, as with Christianity until recently and currently with the IS Caliphate.

Geneticists can become agitated by any suggestion of genetically driven group development or an inherited movement towards altruism or cooperation, so best to remain with inquiries within the realms of social evidence. An assumption that no species could prosper unless it was genetically programmed to propagate, to avoid predators and to find sustenance will not draw criticism these days. Speculation that genes within a group, a flock or a pack, say, may influence behaviour towards cooperation of individuals, or altruism, will draw fire from Dawkins, warning of an irrational side-track here. With *The Selfish Gene* he is keen to exhibit that genes in an individual will influence its carrier to compete against all others exactly because its line of further descent is only by way of its carrier's own offspring, and not others in its tribe.

Dawkins would have us habituated to treating the gene as distinct from the hosting organism. The gene as a replicator, the organism as the vehicle, perhaps vessel may be better. The gene, the replicator, may begin as a parasite, but once the interests of the replicator and the interests of the vessel align, the replicator will not need to work against the interests of the vessel, and will perhaps work for it.

So what of the 'urges' we might find in some species, which look to favour increasing consciousness sharing, cooperation or perhaps altruism? What of those we might recognise in humankind?

Propagation as a primary instinct does not need to engage in any degree of competition for life, simply its absence will make elimination inevitable. The will to survive and prosper led to the tendency toward expansion in hominids more than 200,000 years ago, which Peter Watson notes as the 'Defeat of Cold' so to the use of heating and the development of clothing, otherwise devising opportunities to eliminate occupiers of favorable environments to replace them, or now to invent and fabricate favourable environments to support them. This might be called the Urge to Swarm, which we recognise readily in insects and rodents, but in the present quarter millennium we should judge ourselves as in plague.

Anatomically modern humans descended from a specimen of course called 'Eve' by anthropologists, most likely a variation of *Homo habilis* around 200,000 years ago. Three skulls now held in Ethiopia date from 160,000 years ago. They are three of a world population estimated as between 100,000 and 300,000 individuals, sharing the planet with small groups of *H. erectus* and perhaps 70,000 Neanderthals until 30,000 or so years ago. They all worked with fire, made tools and clothing, but anthropologists are disunited over the extent of language.

Possession of fire and tools did not save Erectus and Neanderthals from extinction, but some skill favoured *sapiens* in the competition for life. Some speculate this was efficient language, enabling information transfer. At the time when humankind reached Australia over the North Landbridge, the several branches of hominid elsewhere made a world population of under one million altogether in small disparate gatherings.

Integrating figures ventured by Peter Watson, the Smithsonian Institute and Canadian Ronald Wright suggest a world hominid population of 100,000 souls at the time of their discovery of fire ignition and tool making. This remained steady over a long period from 9.8 million to 500,000 years ago, rising to 300,000 hominids at the beginning of the Upper Paleolithic, where it remained until the adaptation of husbandry and agriculture, which formed the Neolithic Revolution. About 5000 years later, say 250 generations or so, world population had risen fifty-fold to between 15 million and 20 million. By Year Zero of the Common Era the figure was between 150 million and 330 million.

This suggests that the advent of food-supply domestication increased the rate of fecundity in women and of lifespans, although anthropologists have also noted a lowering of the average height of humankind, perhaps due to a lack of variety from domestication rather than food hunted and gathered. Most scholars express no doubt that improvements in husbandry and agriculture made available the sustenance needed to grow a population. Improvements were made on the wave of information transfer, of the consciousness sharing newly possible with language. Two early sociolinguistics writers, W.D. Whitney in 1875 and H.L. Menken in 1927, remarked on the plasticity of current languages. Since the function of language is expression, perhaps an increasing efficiency in language over the ten millennia to Year Zero CE correlates with advances in production techniques.

An urge to play has a serious intention in the judgement of New York University's Professor Richard Sennett.

Evidence of games worldwide and through time carries to us a suspicion they were with us always, as throwing games, body contest, with weaponry, targeting, stick and ball play that would develop into hockey or cricket or billiards or baseball or lacrosse. Ancient Egyptians had a board game called Senet, ancient India the beginnings of chess and playing cards. An Indian museum exhibits a six-sided rolling dice marked with dots numbering one to six from the Indus Valley dated to 3000 years BCE.

In *The Craftsman*, Sennett lists the first requirement of play as the establishment of functional rules, then practice and repetition. He sees complexities in play as increasing curiosity and encouraging innovation.

'Play is, second, a school for learning to increase complexity.'[26]

Sennett, an urban sociologist, had in mind a modern child, but the ancient child should have learned through play also. Through earlier epochs, play in bodily contest, weapon games or targeting, must have increased agilities for defence, predation and anticipation.

Since knowledge gives advantage, one would expect a behavioral variation towards an urge to curiosity to perpetuate by selection. This was not always so. When consciousness in humankind reached a level capable of highly abstract thought, imagination provided a vivid picture of perils in a world in which change is the constant. In a life that is sustained only by devouring another and, given the puniness of themselves and the grandness of their surroundings, this assumption of a higher and supernatural order must have been unavoidable. This seems to be without exception.

In East Africa hear Ryszard Kapuściński in *Travels with Herodotus*, marvelling at the number of languages, some with a hundred speakers, and hear his cry of wonder at the religions:

> Each tribe has its own unique deities.
> And why should they not have
> started with one god, but right away

---

[26] Richard Sennett, *The Craftsman*, Penguin Books, 2009.

with several? Why does humanity endure for thousands and thousands of years before developing the idea of a single deity? [27]

The histories of which we know are remarkably similar. Once religious supplicants formed associations enough to survive beyond some critical mass, they invited divine instruction, alert for signs in the near physical world, or in the heavens. Appearances to soothsayers that occur reliably in all populations to the immense relief of all congregations, invariably before the development of recording technology, were followed by an enduring divine silence. Then embraced as sacred, so ensuring governance by a class of jurisprudential scholars for as long as religion persists. It is as if we were seeking signs, hoping for instruction, anxious to take refuge in it whatever the source. Rules of sacredness prohibited improvement, unless faith weakened, allowing variation in belief then permitting enquiry. Fear had displaced an urge to curiosity, or its tendency, in favor of an urge to faith. Religion robbed humankind of its heroism.

---

27 Ryszard Kapucśiński, *Travels with Herodotus* (Polish: Podróże z Herodotem), Random House, 2004.

Cooperation as a civil method

Cooperation as a civil method, in performing tasks and equalising returns from effort, makes for advantage in a group beyond family size, but humankind has not come by it readily. Certainly, we observe a keen hatred of cooperative societies from Western commercialist groups in the USA and parts of Europe and Asia, antagonists to China and Cuba and to Russia despite the liquidation of the Soviet Union. This may exhibit a dislike of cooperation covering the means of production, although forced cooperation, slavery, was, until recently, a feature of production techniques worldwide. So the trait favouring individualism remains strong yet. Richard Dawkins explains this in *The Selfish Gene*, where the answer is present in the title. The genetic replicator favours its own host, its vessel, to the exclusion of all others. Cooperation seems to have had an easier ride within a religion, but no further.

With the advent of the Neolithic Revolution, the change to domestication of plants and animals, which took place in various parts of the world at various times, did show some gradual expansion in traits for cooperation in various ways for various cultures.

Changes to local cooperative behaviour over 10,000 years, or say 500 generations, were given insufficient time to excite genetic choice for improvement. Through deep time the genetic system has required millions of years to acculturate. Change in human behavioural patterns towards encouraging cooperation as a civil method may require many more generations to genetically set.

This raises an issue which nudges the ontological. If change in human capacity is caused by a persistent abstract construct, or an institution or idea, or if progress and development in the construct follows replication, variation, advantage, selection, then the avenue for instinctive or trait behaviour becoming set genetically might be overtaken by the advance and persistence in the obeyed construct, so might the biological mechanism become irrelevant?

Because an abstract construct, an idea, propagates by passing from one mind into another, it can pass through many of its own generations speedily, and provide behavioural variations speedily, exponentially faster than a replicator using biology as its pathway. Propagation and variation along the human biological path required thousands of generations to effect and become embedded.

Much human behaviour now is influenced by the repetition of abstract constructs, institutions, methodologies, all of which reproduce speedily merely by passing into the mind of another, so producing variations, advantage, ready for selection. A process along this path may occur at the speed of sound, from a broadcast, say, or during a conversation. This presents a disturbing possibility: Is this ability in abstract vessels to fix in place human behaviour without the need for slow generational inheritance, replacing the biological? Is responsibility for human development now passing to the inanimate?

Not quite yet. Geneticists at the University of Copenhagen in 2018 reported the isolation of a genetic abnormality in the Bajau people, tribes of sea nomads living offshore through the Indonesian Archipelago. They spear fish, for which they dive, capable of spending four or five minutes at depths hundreds of feet below the surface on one breath, lacking buoyancy, they are able to walk the sea floor stalking prey. Each has increased capacity for production of oxygen-carrying red blood cells, enabled by a spleen fifty per cent larger than those of landed neighbours. Anthropologists judge the Bajau have lived as sea communities for around 1000 years, so perhaps twenty or so generations for these variations to occur and select the attribute for success in the struggle for life. And here we may also see the recent progress in abstract thought, with the arrival of rubber-powered spearguns and glass lenses for diving goggles.

We may be saved from the ignominy of biological progress eventually by losing to the inanimate. By the movement in some societies toward the sharing of consciousness, to exchanging empathies, to seeking and providing cooperation as a civil method. Thus, following the lead of all the artistries, to become expressive, with improved chances of success.

Spectacular change is with us now

Spectacular change is with us now through an acquired urge to acknowledge where the increase in production, storage and dissemination of information can justify the word 'explosion'.

Of these three dimensions, the need to share is the most surprising in seeming to run contrary to the genetic instinct to favour the interests of one's host to the disadvantage of all others. And advances in the technologies of dissemination are unwavering in direction; from the time of mimetics, which Merlin Donald so admires, through language, diagram, the artistries, printing, libraries, telegraph, radio, television, computers, the Web and soon quantum computers. The trajectory is astonishing.

Consciousness, the ability to perceive the environment and to best adjust to it, has much increased the capacity now to discover, absorb and broadcast information, enabled by certain classes in our societies that feel a duty to foster enlightenment. This duty, another abstract construct with influence over human behaviour, makes quick progress between minds with a technological bent observed throughout the sciences. Remaining apace with progress sorely tests the mechanisms of communication. Human knowledge doubles every thirteen months, estimates Brian Cox, a professor with the Physics School at Manchester.

The regional imbalance in publication is marked but expected. Following the Thomson Reuters paper of 2009,[28] a table showing the number of scientific papers published in 2013–14 by country, appears on the website of a scientific community. Hosted by the Redditt Company of Massachusetts,[29] this shows the strength of scholarly works through Europe, the Americas and Asia-Pacific, with little appearance from the Middle East, and none from Africa other than South Africa. Per capita publications list first Switzerland, then Denmark, Sweden, Norway, Netherlands, Australia. The USA lies well down, reflecting the diversity of its many societies and access to education.

If the selfish gene favours aggressive individualism, the intensity of its influence is not consistent everywhere.

Social psychologists are currently fond of mapping national cultures using descriptions of social attitudes termed Social Conservatives and Social Liberals in a

---

28 Thomson Reuters, *2009 Journal Citation Reports®* (JCR), June 2010.

29 www.reddit.com/r/dataisbeautiful/comments/20k5dk/top_40_countries_by_the_number_of_scientific/

table titled 'The Psychological Atlas of the World'.[30] The most recent work by Professor Stankov groups many nations in southern Asia, Africa and Latin America as Social Conservative in national temper, and many European countries together with Australia and Canada as Social Liberal. The USA, Russia and China scored between the two. This approach finds tribal Africa and Papua New Guinea difficult to classify. The criteria align Social Conservatism with an individual's traits for resistance to change, admiration of individualism, distrust of cooperative ventures, dislike of tax-funded health and welfare, national pride and resistance to immigrants. Social Liberalism warms to the reverse.

This ignores, but also points out the existence of opposing societies within many national entities, notably the USA, also Britain, Australia, Canada, and some European nations. The political massacre of seventy children by Knight Templar Anders Breivik shows Norway shouldn't be overlooked. In all these political centres we have watched the opposing societies draw a line between them, separating those who support a commercial arena of contestants' antagonism to the success of their competitors. Here empathies become

---

30 Lazar Stankov and Jihyun Lee, 'Toward a Psychological Atlas of the World With Mixture Modeling', *Journal of Cross-Cultural Psychology*, volume 47, issue 2, 28 October 2015.

an impediment, contrasting with those supporting a civilian cooperation, where civil is understood as each member modifying personal demands in the interests of a common good.

This has become the usual political conflict in the Western world. Antipathy between the two sides intensifies as the wealth of the middle classes diminishes, more contestants fall, blaming health and welfare costs, public education expense, graduated tax rates, immigration, foreign ownership. Political electioneering responds in matching tone, to draw fearful voters who are attracted by bellicose tactics, gerrymander, stalemate, the destruction of constitutional conventions, impeachment, fraud, a path toward State Failure.

An aside, but of some importance: if the selfish gene has selected to favour aggressive individualism in males, higher than in females, we might suspect its advantage once lay in promotion of insistent mating, over female resistance. Protective societies struggle, with a civil method or a strong criminal law, to override the genetic impulse to male sexual aggression.

A function of every life

A function of every life is to provide a generation. For much human life the function broadens its reach to include a tendency to reward higher abstract thought, the constructs, the fictions. Advances in human capability, beginning as biological enhancements, run on to function as tools for understanding the world and one another. The opposable thumb, a variation useful for grip in early primates, first functioned for *Homo habilis* in tool making, then in fashioning marks of meaning, then on into our contemporary artistries. The ability to make a loud cry, useful in finding a mate, progressed to the larynx in early hominids then, after mimetics, went on to provide intricacies that became speech and song. Increase in brain size, marked in *Homo erectus,* allowed for an intelligence useful in hunting and avoiding predators, then functioning to provide a facility for enquiry.

Thereafter, the propensity for progress moved to the capacity for the abstract. Religion seems to have established its hegemony early, to which all the social constructs were in fealty: language, diagram, writing, libraries, the early techniques of information storage and supply.

As religions weakened, or permitted enquiry, a syncretic adjustment to engage with the products of curiosity, which is to say knowledge, the momentum advanced the interests of groups, of nations, of the species.

We are observing a proliferation of knowledge now, a commonality of consciousness. What force propels this? Geneticists will be better at drawing the straight lines of causality than other theorists, and they will not all agree. The context now suggests that influences over human behaviour are migrating from the biological to the abstract, likely accelerating variations exponentially. The proliferation of knowledge, and the impulse to share it, set a trajectory toward increasingly effectual consciousness sharing.

All the artistries, the languages of our cultures, have moved in the same direction by taking as their goal an engagement with empathies. A stronger commonality will find countervailing forces. Opposition will continue from the religions, and from the commercialist classes who favour an arena of contestants as the temper of governance, of power.

Does an increase in shared consciousness in human behaviour mirror the function of the biological path to consciousness, which is to say: to better understand our circumstances, to better adjust to them, for increased chance of survival? Might this provide an encouragement to altruism? An embedded urge? A reading of Richard Dawkins' chapter *The Gene Machine* may allow this.

With the influences directing human development

With the influences directing human development migrating from the biological to the abstract, variation as a necessity for evolution must move away from cellular aberration as its source. Abstract aberrations, anomalies, corruption, should provide the pathways to change, as in biology. Corruption in microbes, especially viruses, provides an analogy. To plague the biological being, ruthless life developed parasites, among which viruses are effective in providing variation, changing behaviour of the host, to effect more efficient proliferation.

In times of development in abstract thought, infection by strains of aberration established an Emperor obsession, where previously peaceful neighbours of nation states warred to control one another and expand their power. First recorded seems to be the Lagash under Eannatum in 2500 BCE Mesopotamia, giving way to the Akkadian, with Sargon the Great, two centuries later. A related obsession is modern worldwide in the condition of hyper greed, particularly plain among the few owners of today's Manhattan, whose guiding compulsion feels no need of public office, preferring the influence of immense wealth. Obsessions with the sacred, with sorcery, religions, slavery, racial and gender hatred, prove persistent, awaiting successful variation.

Each component of a culture defends against variation as best it can, the lesser ever vulnerable to displacement by invasion. In the New World and in Australia we saw the dominant culture destroy the invaded, first the hierarchy, then the artistries, then the languages. This freed the defeated from the bonds of culture to provide the possibility of variation and freedom to build on enquiry, and its product: knowledge. Recovery is a slow process. So far, invading powers have kept the invaded ignorant, but this may be a losing tactic. In the US, Australia and Africa the powerful have feared knowledge in the displaced and denied them education. In Africa, we now see suggestions that entrenched powerful groups are providing politicians to govern who are of less capacity than those below.

Knowledge makes for advantage, a clearly sufficient imperative for our species to select this capacity, where it can, and therefore develop an expanding intelligence.

Consciousness

Consciousness may be thought a synonym for the ability to sense circumstances and best adjust to them. Knowledge makes for advantage, in the struggle for life, which seems to provide consciousness with its function, its reason for being.

Recognition of this by rationalist thinkers led to modern evolutionary theory, weakening the authority of religion in ethics and morality. Today most subscribe to some form of Benthamist utilitarianism and the choice of a greater good, to encourage proliferation and happiness, while inhibiting destruction, pain and misery. Fine definitions of good can be elusive; the contributions from Moore, Murdoch, Kant, Wittgenstein, Singer, with many others, fill volumes. Following a path set by evolutionary theory can provide a satisfying secular ethic and offer an attractive resurrection of the ancient religious struggle between good and evil.

The path blazed by evolutionary enquiry invites progression to this secular ethic, in line with the evolutionary progression, to produce and sustain life and advance the species: with development of consciousness, most likely beginning in the single-celled microbes, came the ability to recognise circumstances, and best adjust to them; with development of abstract thought came the tenet that knowledge makes for advantage between species, and between individuals, in competition.

The path knowledge may be expected to use, so as to make for advantage, may indicate some possibilities we might favour as a secular ethic, and some not. Entitled to be classed as knowledge, information should be highly graded for authenticity, Plato's passionate plea, avoiding the spurious or misleading. Methods of storage and transmission lie along the route to advantage. So ready access to knowledge will be highly scored by an ethicist, and easy retrieval from storage of knowledge in uncontaminated form. In pursuit of knowledge extension, presumption of further hypotheses is already a technique central to the practice of scientific enquiry. As is the testing of hypotheses for falsifiability, Karl Popper's plea.

Enquiry should be free from doctrines imposed by religion or political scripture. Moses' tablets, Hadith, Sruti, Gospel, and Mao's Little Red Book, with their libraries, were designed to entrench the sacred, protect it from deviation, prohibit change. Neither error nor improvement is possible. The imperative, change, as a condition precedent to improvement was recognised by Darwin, Wallace, Huxley, and other evolutionists. An earlier trace can be found in the late 1790s with Kant's enquiry into the nature of judgement in humankind, noting that accurate judgement of beauty can be achieved only when uncontaminated by social forces. He proposed the facility for judgement as a fundamental component of human rationality. Had he considered consciousness as a capacity for sensing one's conditions and best adjusting to them, a choice that requires judgement, he may have found his argument simpler.

Slavery continues

Slavery continues its popularity as a benefit for the owners, in parts of the world into the 21st century, despite the pain and misery which is its objective. It continues in regions of the Christian Central Americas where animist tribes are compulsorily indentured to Christian land clearers. And in the Middle East where Islamic State proponents justify enslavement of unbelieving women and children by reference to Hadith, which also call for the genocide of all male unbelievers, indeed wherever they are found in the world. Many Hadith, including quotations attributed to Abu Said al-Khudri, appeared in the IS publication *Dabiq* to promote slavery, and the rape of slaves and captives, in 2013.

The American Civil War in the mid-18th century was fought over slavery by the Abolitionist states against the Confederate slave-owning states. Although southern historians increasingly reclassify the dispute as states' rights. August 2017 saw the riots following white supremacist rallies in Charlottesville Virginia, one of several states where movements in support of black subservience remain strong.

A society in which death is the result of the refusal to work for a power holder may count itself a slave state. Those societies that regard themselves as post slavery – most of the Americas, much of Africa, Oceania and notably Australia – should be unsettled by modern trends in tax policies.

The inflation of personal wealth held by an ever-concentrating few hyper rich, concurrently throughout the West and some Southeast Asian nations, proceeds in lockstep with their demands for reductions in their tax burden. In those nations with ageing populations, provision of funding for government expenditure, including aged care and health care, falls on the younger earners.

As more of the means of production is taken by the minority of hyper rich, allowing savings from cost cutting and extinguishing duplication, so shrinks the middle class, enlarging the unemployment pool, lowering labour demand and labour costs. This suits the warfare economies, making military service attractive for a larger proportion of the population.

For example, a pie chart produced in 2018 showing classes of expenditure for the USA allots 67 per cent of total national expenditure to military. Military service carries welfare rewards. By contrast, Germany's greatest expenditure is in welfare, around one third of its total budget. During 2018 the *New York Times* reported a social rivalry developing between 'The Aged v the Young' over the nation's ability to meet its welfare needs, and the burden the young now face for the care of the old. Australia looks set to take the US route, proposing taxation relief for its largest commercial corporations.

Those economies in which capital takes the feudal path, concentrating wealth and denying welfare, lead the majority of their populations back to slavery. Unless rebellion intervenes.

Uncoupling morality from the gods

Uncoupling morality from the gods is a task that can be recognised in societies at the time of David ruling Israel and Judah, say a millennium BCE. Psalm 14 speaks of disbelievers citing the incapability of God, whose works are abominable, who cannot improve the fortunes of the destitute.

God's shortfalls caused little consternation in the later West, and most societies were content to ascribe human development to supernatural planning. The modern movement of focus from the spiritual to the physical was to be disturbing. Charles Darwin was disturbed by it, as was his wife Emma, who feared impiety may separate them in the afterlife. *On the Origin of Species* was to elevate, above the biblical values, consideration of the components or our existence.

A secular morality

A secular morality, if we recognise one, should have no trouble selecting against slavery so to avoid pain and suffering in humankind, but not solely because of this. The practice of slavery works against variability as an agent of evolutionary progress in both the slaver society and the enslaved. And the pressure for improvement in the skills of abstract thought and enquiry is almost absent in the slave-holding class which, in the Americas, was seen to decay, weakening it in conflict.

Most, perhaps all, arguments in favour of slavery, East and West, depend on holy scripture, and those based on racial supremacy rely on religious support as a second tier of contention.

Hypotheses in explanation of the natural world, or the psychological, supported by scripture and equally by established rational knowledge are hard to find. Often to justify a term the use of scripture to support a hypothesis indicates that the argument is without support from sources of rational enquiry or an established body of knowledge.

Have we reached a point in the development of rationality that treats religious support for a proposal as evidence of falsity? Not quite. Exercise of compassion and empathies, usefully increasing a volume of knowledge, is encouraged by evolutionist learning and by some scriptures. However, the incidence of repudiation in social practice is high. Repudiation of altruism has some influential champions, as Ayn Rand has shown.

The possibility of perfection within reach of 'all corporeal and mental endowments' of existing beings was attractive to Darwin and was 'produced by laws acting around us'. These laws, which we might term, nearly 200 years later, 'algorithms' govern evolutionary progress. Paul Davies, in *About Time*, is sceptical of 'self-organising processes' in nature leading to 'organisational complexity' and the inevitable improvement of species and individuals. Increasing complexity may not be an end in itself but the shape of the progress of change produces effects that are regressive and die out, or advantageous and succeed. This begins slowly then increases exponentially. Notwithstanding Davies' caution, improvement in performance and influence of humankind over recent millennia is inescapably evident. The tone of Darwin's final sentence in his marvellous Chapter XIV in *On the Origin of Species* is warm:

> There is a grandeur in this view of life, with its several powers, having been originally breathed into a few forms, or into one, and that, whilst this planet has gone cycling on according

to the fixed law of gravity, from so simple a beginning endless forms most beautiful and most wonderful have been, and are being, evolved.

Development of abstract thought

Development of abstract thought, where some forms of symbol substitute for simple actuality, leads to imagination. Just as knowledge makes for advantage, so does the capacity to recognise other possibilities, the building blocks of contingent reasoning, of conjecture.

An aside, but of interest here: knowledge making for advantage is not a mechanism useful to those species relying on biological improvement rather than intellectual. Some insects have made their advances taking advantage of short life spans. This speeds along the rate of variation and selection of biological alternatives in pursuit of success. Two spectacular examples are species of ants. The Central American Leafcutter lives in colonies of many million individuals, building underground nests nearly 50 metres square with tunnels, chambers, nurseries, waste dumps, and food factories producing leaf fungus for food and antibiotics against infections. A South American Fire Ant colony is typically a thousand individuals who lock themselves together to float as a pad in flood times, the lower breathing air from captive bubbles, the colony behaving as a pouring fluid or as a solid as it chooses. Both species seem to behave cooperatively as if directed by a single shared consciousness.

Species that rely on the products of enquiry for success, ourselves and those we fabricate, benefit from longevity to increase investigation, validate, and improve judgement as well as we are able.

Are we on track to propose elements which a secular ethic will require? This may encourage recognition of circumstances, choice and judgement to beneficially adjust, to allow anticipation, far sightedness. Continuous enquiry, so to increase the volume of knowledge, and ready access to this knowledge, may be counted as good, restrictions on access as evil, as with perversion of established knowledge and obfuscation. Sacredness, intransigence, so to prevent variations, might be considered an evil, making for disadvantage. Free enquiry as its converse is seen as a good.

Principles of selection, working to favour improvement, act to disadvantage the losers in the struggle for life, a doom Darwin termed 'the Extinction of less-improved forms'. Some social movements have had, and some have now, an intention to speed the process along, eliminating those seen as 'less-improved forms' by sterilisation, banishment, ethnic cleansing, genocide. Many of these movements have been religious, but not all.

Moralities based on religion are unlikely to evolve, since they are generally caught by sacredness, and fixed in expression and effect. Secular moralities will find progress and evolvement more easily. In those societies that permit secular moralities, a vanguard of progress toward intensified empathy, and sympathy for the plight of victims, have left the older moral standards far behind. Nowhere are these advances more obvious than in the histories of invasions, slavery, and colonisations, where modern sympathies are for the pitiful overrun.

Ireland's servitude as a vassal state began in the 1100s with incursions by the English, and more briefly the Normans, at a time when the English ruling classes justified it as a highly moral venture against heathen outlanders and were supported by Pope Adrian IV. English antipathy to the Irish grew with the movement to the Church of England, while the Irish majority remained Catholic, so English sympathy for Ireland's plight through the Irish famines of the 1800s remained slight through to the 1900s when Irish resistance to English dominance was put down ruthlessly by English military and the secret paramilitaries. But so far had English moral empathies progressed by 2011 that Queen Elizabeth II in a speech from Dublin Castle was moved to review her nation's eight centuries of fierce subjugation: 'With the benefit of historical hindsight we can all see things which we would wish had been done differently, or not at all.'

The British Queen's understanding of the advances in ethical standards over time was well ahead of her colonies'. In Australia, an Indigenous movement for constitutional recognition as part recompense for the loss of their lands was dismissed by Prime Minister Howard. The more moralities evolve to keep pace with current knowledge and sensitive empathies, the more disgruntled will become those who prefer a fixed, historical standard of judgement.

A contemporary search for a secular morality

A contemporary search for a secular morality that follows the evolutionary clues to improvement must take account of development, beyond the biological forces, to the intellectual in human behaviour. The influences here are abstract constructs, institutions, arrangements, ideas, all generated by the phenomenal growth in capacity for abstract thought. We have empowered abstract vessels, ideas, to rearrange patterns of human behaviour without the need for slow generational inheritance, so supplanting the biological progressions. A most spectacular product of the loss of biological influence, to the advantage of the intellectual, is selective management for advantage in the competition for life. From grooming for fleas, through Neolithic domestication of plants and animals, through medicine and surgery, to genetic engineering.

Much of this work is presently in food production, medicines and vaccines, some in pollution snares like enhanced trees, and draws little criticism from ethicists because it is in the interests of improvement or as defence against parasites. Perhaps bravado is the danger here. As in the cloning of the sheep Dolly, which points to the philosophical problem that the process of cloning prohibits variation, therefore improvement, acting against the progress for which we hope. A remarkable feature of our so-far existence.

Perils of laboratory bravado disturbed Yuval Noah Harari at the Hebrew University in Jerusalem. He was goaded by the invention of a fluorescent rabbit by Brazilian Eduardo Kac in the year 2000. South Korean laboratories, since then, have issued into the world a number of fluorescent cats. Harari wondered where experimentation might lead, perhaps to the re-designing of humankind. In 2014, in *Sapiens* he wrote, 'Tinkering with our genes won't necessarily kill us. But we might fiddle with *Homo sapiens* to such an extent that we would no longer be *Homo sapiens*.'

Tinkering in the laboratory provides the Darwinian requirement for the possibility of improvement, which is to say variation, but may inhibit the operation of natural selection by success in the struggle for life. Typically now, success is judged by performance in a commercial market, which may sound a warning to all humankind.

Evolutionary paths to a secular ethic

Evolutionary paths to a secular ethic, enabled by increased capacity for abstract thought, have led through the primacy of enquiry, to favour free access to knowledge, presentation of information in a truthful form, frequent testing for fallacy, resistance to secrecies and prohibitions.

This may not bring us to a point of ready cooperation with one another, to an effort to achieve a common good, to a rejection of the antagonistic model of society, were it not for the influence within modern societies of our artistries. They stand against a regression into another Dark Age, the return to domination and subjugation that threatens at the time of writing. The artforms now display moment toward empathies as their path toward shared expression, a commonality of consciousness, and our understanding of one another, our perception of our circumstances, our adjustment to them. And this is true of every artistry, East and West.

The effective mechanism was the phenomenon of shared consciousness between the artist, or the performer, or the writer, and their audience, this need for emotional transfer, active empathies, accelerating to and through the present time. The beginnings seem to lie far in antiquity. Guessing the point of birth of an artistry we rely on such evidence as has survived. Evidence of the incorporeal arts, for example song, has survived in oral traditions more clearly than the physical, which we have lost to decay.

Many evolutionists believe humankind began among proto-human societies that already used language, so was born song. Verbal and rhythmic artistries, song, dance, music, were early taken over by the religions everywhere, to serve their gods and their priests, then released to public use only as the grasp of the sacred weakened. In the West this was Classical Greece, where the gods were left to bicker amongst themselves, while intellectualism among the high-born became concerned with secular ethics, principles of proper governance, and refinement of communication, which is to say aesthetics. This movement, dormant during fundamentalist Christianity, has begun a recovery only recently, encouraged by the emergence of evolutionism.

If we take the path to empathies offered by the artistries as a component of a secular ethic, we should increase our chances of progress to safety and happiness, avoiding destruction, lessening pain and misery in ourselves and in others, as possible with all compatible life forms, reaching for Darwin's 'grandeur in this view of life'.

In *The Descent of Man,* Darwin came close to judging empathies and cooperation as pinnacles of a secular ethic.

> The social instincts, which no doubt were acquired by man as by the lower animals for the good of the community, will from the first have given to him some wish to aid his fellows, some feeling of sympathy, and have compelled him to regard their approbation and disapprobation. Such impulses will have served him at a very early period as a rude rule of right and wrong.

Empathy offers an inviting path to enhanced knowledge and, if one leans to a view that a central function of consciousness is the aggregation and transfer of knowledge, an empathist understanding the circumstances of the other should sit comfortably with this.

Absence of evolutionary theory

Absence of evolutionary theory from our search for a feasible secular morality is remarkable. Philosophy's library shelves are bare here.

From ancient philosophy to the present, arguments attempting the separation of morality from religion were not united in their choice of premises. From Plato we have the use of the sun as a metaphor for the production of light; from Earl Russell the hope of a solution from mathematics; from Murdoch the 'Obscurity of Good' is an opaque attempt but she tried hard; from Sartre the 'nauseousness of freedom'; Camus never found his 'moral order'.

Charles Darwin returned from his voyages with a reassessment of time, of the processes of geological change, of biological progression, and the rules that life seems to follow in order to prosper, and liberated intellectual enquiry from its godly necessity. Yet none has ever caught the light for moral philosophers.

In the USA, where social pressure in favour of religion is high, any search for feasible secular ethics is absent. Even the online *Stanford Encyclopaedia of Philosophy* has no entry for this in its Table of Contents. Australia, a more sceptical society, has produced Peter Singer, who classifies himself as an atheist utilitarian dealing in competing social interests. Raimond Gaita prefers a path to ethics focused on one wronging another.

So to Russia, where moral philosophy provides a surprise. Principles of secularism have lost primacy. Government has drawn in the traditional religions, Christianity, Judaism, Islam and Buddhism, in a moral partnership, so social values promoted by them are now supported by government, thus strengthening support for the regime under Vladimir Putin, who describes social diversity as 'God given'. Nicolai Petro of the University of Rhode Island writes of this:

> Finally in today's Russia the Orthodox Church is closely partnered with the state. It provides both intellectual and moral support to many state policies, not because it has to, but because it wants to.[31]

---

31 Nicolai Petro, 'Russia's Moral Framework', *The National Interest*, 24 September 2015.

One might have expected a secular society

One might have expected a secular society, as is China, to have worked on the rational development of a secular morality, but the tradition is otherwise. Chinese philosophical practice keeps sternly away from a search for neglected first principles. The Confucians, and later others, are much more inclined to choose a path set by the epiphanies of sages. This has remained true after the Communist Revolution. Of the Party philosophers, Zhou Enlai laid down Four Modernisations to guide China's next development, and reformist Deng Xiaoping followed this path, establishing Four Cardinal Principles: 'Upholding the basic spirit of Communism, Upholding the People's democratic dictatorship political system, Upholding the leadership of the Communist Party.' And the fourth, in the tradition of the epiphanies of the sages: 'Upholding Marxism, Leninism and Mao Zedong Thought.'[32]

Addition of Xi Jinping Thought may follow.

Contemporary Chinese philosophers are drawn to begin an analysis of political morality with a commitment to the Dictatorship of the Proletariat. Since China is to date the most successful society to overthrow tyrannical subjugation of a people, we may become resigned to acceptance of its choice. Schools of Chinese philosophy seem now to split between Chinese Buddhism, whose prime sage is the Gautama Buddha, the neo-Confucians, and the New Left whose prime sages are Marx, Lenin and Mao Zedong. The new Left is currently in the ascendancy, led by Wang Hui. Prohibitions are many and opportunities for variation, therefore for improvement, are few so evolutionist ethicists will fear the narrowing of opportunities. The answers to questions of political behaviour are to be found, as ever, within the culture.

---

32 Deng Xiaoping, 'Four Cardinal Principles', *China Internet Information Center*, 22 June 2011 (March 1979).

The algorithm

The algorithm that bore us requires death as a necessary step in the competition for life. Death of a generation enables the next. No species strives to defeat its algorithm with as much intensity as does humankind. Medical sciences have extended the world's human life expectancy from fifty years in 1900 to over eighty years in many countries now, on US National Institute on Aging figures.[33] Japan is the current leader at eighty-three years, and fastest growth in expectancy presently is in underdeveloped regions, evidence of an insistent impulse to perpetuity, the unattainable goal.

One's being persists in one's consequences, true of all life, most poignantly in humankind.

A list of contributors of consequence in human progress might begin with our common ancestor *Homo erectus* 'Eve', who gave birth to the variation that raised *Homo sapiens*, beginning our 10,000 generations so

---

33 See www.nia.nih.gov/sites/default/files/2017-06/global_health_aging.pdf and other National Institute on Aging reports.

far, estimated by Ronald Wright.³⁴ Thereafter the histories lack women until time reaches Nefertiti around 1331 BCE, then Cleopatra VII Philopator, say 300 generations later.

Since writing began, we have come to enjoy more vivid and detailed accounts of contributors and their worthiness. Most emperors, royal and religious figures fall short in contributions to the common good, although Jesus Christ, the Prophet Mohammed and the Gautama Buddha made their effort. When time reached beyond 100,000 years or so after 'Eve' and around 500 years before the birth of Cleopatra, the philosopher Thales of Miletus's principle of enquiry shines briefly, until piety again quashes reason. In 5th century BCE Chinese began instruction in logical responsibility for their own actions to the beat of Confucius' ethical regime. The West waited another 120 generations after Miletus for Charles Darwin, Alfred Wallace and Robert Chambers to return to the principle of rational enquiry.

A pantheon able to contain memorials to the illustrious dead, the contributors of great consequence to humankind, must await quantum computing or its successors, but a tome in the imagination might justly begin with a Greek, perhaps Archimedes, carrying on to the many polymaths of their Classical period.

---

34 Ronald Wright, *A Short History of Progress*, Text, 2004.

The addition of a few later minds might bring a warm admiration when uttering some noble names: Virgil, Ptolemy, Abbasid al-Nasir, Dante, Leonardo, Copernicus, Galileo, Newton, Marx, Gandhi, Tagore, Nightingale, Curie, Einstein, Ho Chi Minh, Mandela, suggesting Ancestor Thanksgiving might be better justified as a religion than its competitors allow.

These are contributors to a commonality of consciousness, an understanding of the world and of each another, in a form available to all, bringing gifts to enrich our fleeting lives.

> If the purpose of a life
> is to provide generation, the duty's done.
> And so to death.
> A full life ends content, the race's run.
> Pleased to have bided here my while,
> now my grateful and my final smile.
>
> *John Bryson*

References

Becker, Hal B., 'Can users really absorb data at today's rates tomorrow?', *Data Communications*, July 1986.

Bounie, David & Gille, Laurent, 'International Production and Dissemination of Information: Results, Methodological Issues, and Statistical Perspectives', *International Journal of Communication*, volume 6, 2012.

Chalmers, David J., *The Character of Consciousness*, Oxford University Press, 2010.

Chalmers, David J., *The Conscious Mind: In Search of a Fundamental Theory,* Oxford University Press, 1996.

Christiansen, Morten H & Kirby, Simon (eds), *Language Evolution*, Oxford Studies in the Evolution of Language, Oxford University Press, 2003.

Darwin, Charles, *On the Origin of Species*, John Murray, 1859.

Darwin, Charles, *The Descent of Man*, John Murray, 1871.

Davies, Paul, *About Time*, Viking, 1995.

Dawkins, Richard, *The Selfish Gene*, Oxford University Press, 1976.

Dennett, Daniel, *From Bacteria to Bach and Back: The Evolution of Minds*, W.W. Norton & Company, 2017.

Donald, Merlin, *Origins of the Modern Mind: Three stages in the evolution of culture and cognition*, Harvard University Press, 1991.

Dunbar, Robin (ed.) et al., *Lucy to Language: The Benchmark Papers*, Oxford University Press, 2014.

Dunbar, Robin, *Human Evolution*, Pelican Books, 2014.

Dutton, Denis, *A Darwinian Theory of Beauty*, TED Talk, TED, 15 February 2010.

Godfrey-Smith, Peter, 'Environmental Complexity and the Evolution of Cognition', in R. Sternberg & J. Kaufman (eds), *The Evolution of Intelligence*, Lawrence Erlbaum Associates, 2001.

Godfrey-Smith, Peter, *The Function of the Mind in Nature*, Cambridge University Press, 2005.

Harari, Yuval Noah, *Sapiens*, Vintage Books, 2014.

Heaney, Seamus, *Open Ground: Selected poems, 1966–1996*, Farrar, Straus & Giroux, 1999.

Hutton, James, *The Theory of the Earth*, 2 volumes, London, 1795.

Kapuściński, Ryszard, *Travels with Herodotus* (Polish: *Podróże z Herodotem*), Random House, 2004.

Lawrence, Peter, *Road Belong Cargo: A Study of the Cargo Movement in the Southern Madang District, New Guinea*, Waveland Press, 1989.

Llardo, Melissa, et al., 'Physiological and genetic adaptations to diving in sea nomads', *Cell*, volume 173, issue 3, pp 569–580, 19 April 2018.

Low, Tim, *Where Song Began*, Penguin Books, 2014.

Mack, Katie, 'Recreating the beginning of time', *Cosmos*, 29 June 2015.

McPhee, John, *Basin and Range*, Farrar Straus Giroux, 1981.

Menken, H.L., *Prejudices*, The Library of America, 1919–1927.

Nabokov, Vladimir, *Lectures on Literature*, Harcourt Brace Jovanovich, 1980.

Pareroultja, Kristian, MS 4628, The Schøyen Collection, www.schoyencollection.com

Penrose, Roger, 'On the Gravitization of Quantum Mechanics 1: Quantum State Reduction', *Foundations of Physics*, volume 44, number 5, pp 557–575, 2014.

Petro, Nicolai, 'Russia's Moral Framework', *The National Interest*, 24 September 2015.

Pew Research Centre, 'The Future of World Religions: Population Growth Projections', *2010–2050 Report*, 2 April 2015.

Plante, Thomas B., 'Do We Need Religion to be Ethical?', *Psychology Today*, 28 March 2011.

Plato, *Republic*, c 380 BCE.

Popper, Karl, *The Logic of Scientific Discovery*, 2nd edition, Routledge, 2002.

Schrödinger, E., English translation in R. Chetrite, P. Muratore-Ginanneschi, K. Schwieger, 'E. Schrödinger's 1931 paper "On the Reversal of the Laws of Nature"', *The European Physical Journal H.*, volume 46, number 28, 2021.

Searle, John R., *The Rediscovery of the Mind*, MIT Press, 1992.

Sennett, Richard, *The Craftsman*, Penguin Books, 2009.

Stankov, Lazar, et al., 'Two dimensions of psychological country-level differences', *Learning and Individual Differences*, volume 30, February 2014, pp 22–33.

von Humboldt, Alexander, *Personal Narrative*, 7 volumes, 1819–1829, W. Pople, London, 1939.

Wade, Nicholas, *The Faith Instinct*, Penguin Books, 2010.

Watson, Peter, *Ideas: A History of Thought and Invention, from Fire to Freud*, Harper Perennial, 2006.

Whitney, William Dwight, *The Life and Growth of Language*, first published 1875, Cambridge University Press, 2013.

Wright, Ronald, *A Short History of Progress*, Text, 2004.

Forest- 1/8
RLP

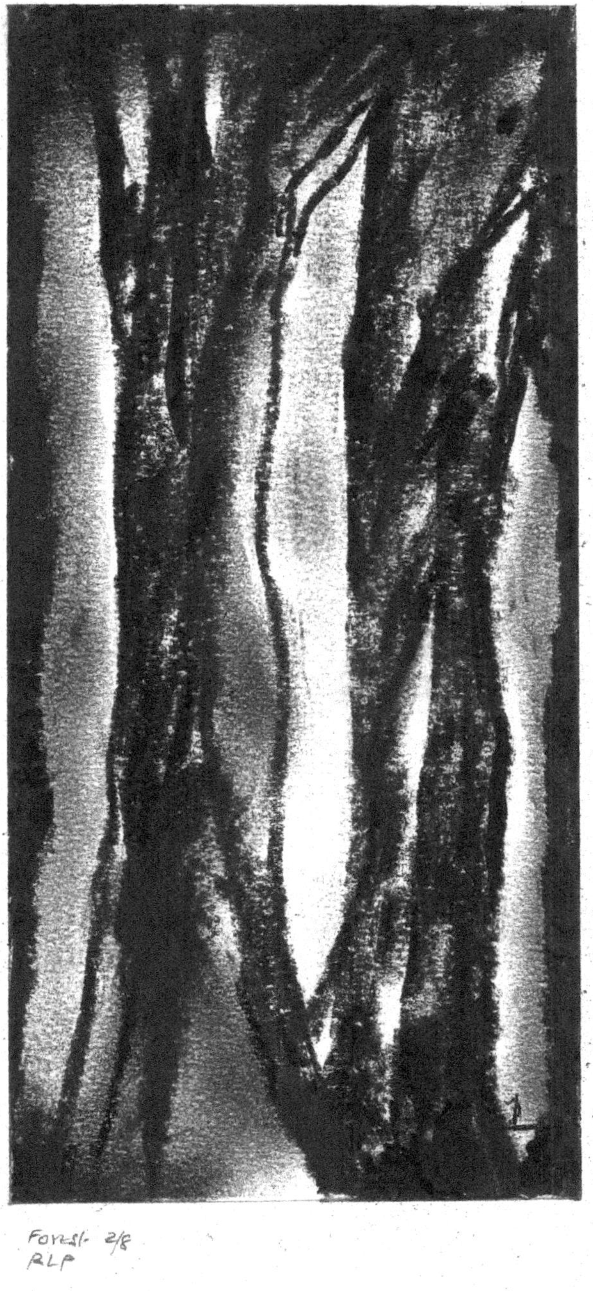

Forest 2/8
RLP

Forest 3/8
RLP

John's poems

Notes on the poems

The idea of collecting John's unpublished poetry in a posthumous book came to Therese and some of us, their friends, during a visit to John in hospital, one of the last. The plan was to choose from all his poems that we could assume were 'finished', as if John were still in our group, guiding us throughout.

Paolo Totaro

Inspired by Paolo's suggestion, we have included some of John's poems in this book. Paolo also led the selection process. While going through the poems, there was endless communication between Paolo and me. We were drawn to the possibility that John was with us in a way, encouraging us as we chose the poems to publish in this collection.

Therese O'Neill

An age of unsteady progress

One evening, separated by a vast distance, Paolo Totaro and John Bryson each tripped and fell to the ground, sustaining injury. They will refrain in future from collaborating on any poem which might again provide the gods with an excuse to play with their fortunes.

For Paolo Totaro

My close friend and I
have reached the Age of Falling,
neither he nor I complaining.
Soon to an Age of Forgetting,
we will, perhaps together,
reach an Age of Reminiscing.
Caught hard on a stair, descending,
by a step somehow missing,
he fell, spent weeks recovering.
His stern eye took in my greeting.
'Who will write whose obituary
is not yet settled,' he said, finding
this uncertainty pleasing.

John Bryson, 13 November 2014

For John Bryson

John, I wish that you, Fidelio and I
would board a boat that sailed
by willpower alone under kindly stars,
and, with no freak wave or wind.
would take us beyond Good Hope,
serene, and when the sweet dream
of Therese and Pippi necessarily arose,
the glowing clouds would become
stage stairs and, in garden clothes,
majestic the two spouses would climb
down from the Paradise we once shared.
'Or maybe not,' they would quietly say,
finding this uncertainty pleasing.

Paolo Totaro, 13 November 2014

On greater age

Of age great enough to draw greetings year on year,
my thanks to all and all and all,
I'm yet too young to draw down on the wages of fear,
but I'm taken by an absurd belief
when my time to leave is come,
I'll miss you all, every last one
whose life ever brushed mine, and will find in death's relief
its sharp poignancy, the keenest nostalgia, not least in my own.

Were we shearwaters, a meridian

So, veer the glide-path, sway, and (here
I use the term as navigators might)
fishtail, a proper quality of asymmetric flight,
in case you're drawn to think we merely fly amok
as Malays say, when I'd rather have it plain enough,
the make of a wave, the ebb of a trough
we hunt apart, but with a tidy sense of flock.
North, then, the vapour way, and clear
into the very iris of the sky
where sometimes eagles stall; another mote
among a hundred thousand, full and by, aswarm
where the senses thin, and all we know is warm
in the genes, or what we've fledgling learned by rote,
it's even in the tricky nature of the light
to chart the doldrum girth (as if it were a cold blue)
with nothing small enough to size the world by
here, so only the infinities can possibly hold true.

Ko Tupapaku Tapu
Lying in state

Now you are sacred
the dew will bathe you,
the moon will paint you
and turn your cloak
to plume and blossom
as your rank deserves.
We can speak later.
Send word: in birdsong
wind-lisp, throaty brook;
make mist, rainbows,
and listen, listen
for my often prayer.

William John O'Meally, flogged

Heave against the sweating iron bands,
arch to meet the whisper of the lash,
the lusting sigh of each successive draw
breathes the ardour of the stroke before.

Bitterness, we understand;
jealousies, anger, hate.
More terrifying,
the thoughtful cruelties
of our inexorable State.

Running wild our endless littered streets,
spattered midnight puke and jai-yard rust,
whose half-tame child looks up, retreats?
Gagging at the stench of our disgust.

Painting fish

Paused, at a stilled pool,
Reprise an often wish,
To watch the gifted child
Painting such colours
On the scales of fish.

This fallen leaf
Walking the Tjumpuhan Valley, Ubud

Wander the gardens, choose a mossy path
beside a lilypad pool where
wavering fish lie in the shade of a glissy bloom,
pass beneath two black butterflies
in endless spirals of lovemaking,
through doors in a pavilion carved
to vast battle scenes of the Ramayana,
wade the pebbled stream which mimics
a meander of the river below,
under starlight frangipani and sunset hibiscus,
beyond the frothy spout of a stone hog's snout
or a frog with a flower behind an ear,
a fetch of glide and swirl,
a hundred strides to the far bank
where geckos drink, a clear view
of the jungle terraces climbing
from riverbend to mountaintop:
waterfalls, treefalls, palm fronds, fern fronds,
weighty tresses of climbers, lacing it together, tight,
there a cicada, pollinating blossom with its dusty tongue
is the one movement to catch the eye here,
where the surge to begin life is so dense
to be uncountable in the space
occupied by a river stone, or beneath this fallen leaf.

Written in Tjumpuhan Valley, Ubud

From a voyage

1. Into a postcard scene, tropic lagoon,
   Palm fronds freehand, glossy horizon,
   steps the ageing writer tended
   by his divorcee daughter,
   her twin godsons at side
   who don't suspect how the
   word 'Rest' panics the old.

2. Floating the lagoon I saw
   weightless on the reef below
   a single sheet of written paper.
   Within a breath's reach it puffed
   into pale cloud at my fingertip
   before I could grasp a word,
   but I was taken hard by the belief
   it carried the first lines of a novel
   or at least a sonnet.

3. Poolside at a resort, watching newly lovers
   at play, and first-time mothers tender, he feels
   an urge to call to them all: 'What events
   you have in store, what astonishing times,'
   but his daughter has adjusted his deck chair
   and the moment is gone.

Of Waratah Bay

Tide's gone. Marching the slow draining strand,
two hundred divisions of soldier crabs
strike the colours. Here's a ruby winkle
drawing, with a finger, a confident ampersand,
though maybe simply lost, and a featherbone
from a cuttlefish who out-flew it; the footfalls
of a dancing child, and the palmprints
from a swaggering seagull's handstand.
The bay sweeps, there, half the world's edge
and at the steepest point I saw a girl
fishing from a hand-painted granite ledge.
Follow her gaze down, so looking up again
the sky's a mirror, and about her line
silver bream flutter and wheel
as if she's hung, from their own ceiling,
a curious and glittery mobile.

September and September

Waiting on war
we crowd the stadium
for a final
already a flop,
in the bleachers
watching the play
of Auden's grim dictum,
see 'those to whom
evil is done do evil in return,'
and hunker down
waiting for the siren.

16th June 2014, Iraq

After massacre by holy warriors, in fervent heat,
of all their prisoners, to the cry 'God is Great,'
might a stealthy doubt occur to those
perhaps in their own sometime death throes:
God is less great for the vengeant shout,
and for the sacrifice, than He was without?

Hatchlings

Mine owners living in the city penthouses,
Import showman Monkton
a viscount and ignoble sceptic,
who advises a takeover of the media
to rule the world.

Through the blue chambers of Lovett Bay
glides a vast turtle, whose mother
was there when Flinders
first chanced the Entrance, so
she understands the rhythms
of the natural world.

Decades on, what vapours
Will her hatchlings breath?

Whakamarumaru

E atua,
Tiaki ratou O whare tenei

Ake ake, no te mea
Ratou pai. Ae.

An exorcism

O spirits,
Protect these people of this house

For all time, because
These people are good. Yes.

Even beyond life

In another life, my love,
From our palace bed, my love,
We'll watch the golden dawn come up
On the walls of the Taj Mahal.

Even beyond life, my love,
Please never be far from me.

On another day, my love,
To the Andes peaks, my love,
On feathered shoes with wings we'll fly
We'll dance at the Sun God's feast.

Even beyond life, my love,
Please never be far from me.

On another day, my love,
Under tall white sails, my love,
Come follow the evening star
To the islands of blue lagoons.

Even beyond life, my love,
Please never be far from me.

In another life, my love,
We'll give thanks for love, my love,
And for the loveless of the world
We'll hold each other's hand and weep.

Even beyond life, my love,
Please never be far from me.

Epilogue

As I come to write this epilogue, I know John would be completely happy with this book.

I had no idea what I was taking on to publish it, on top of widowhood. The depth of loss ... of a partnered way of life, domestic rhythms, a unit completely enmeshed. Everything about where we live was about a shared future. Grief's isolating.

Throughout this journey I had sense of John guiding me, in the air and on the water. The friends he chose to support me were extraordinary – Paolo Totaro AM, Richard Leplastrier AO, Margot Hutcheson, and others. Miraculously, I found Bernadette Foley, from Broadcast Books. What a team. Thank you, thank you, this would not be what it is without you.

Therese O'Neill

Forest 7/8
RLP

About the drawings

John and Therese's friend and neighbour, Richard Leplastrier AO, generously provided his powerful, beautiful drawings to accompany John's writing in these pages..

Richard drew these works for the exhibition *Eucalyptusdom*, held at the Powerhouse Museum, Sydney, in 2022. For more information see https://powerhouse.com.au/program/eucalyptusdom

On the cover is a portrait of John that Richard drew in July 2023 for this book. It is drawn in pencil and charcoal on tracing paper.

> John Bryson lived in Gaimaraigal country, the west side of Pittwater, where the giant spotted gum forest overhangs the emerald green of this quiet estuary. Much of his poetry and these charcoal drawings have sprung from here. They belong together.
>
> *Richard Leplastrier, 2023*

John Bryson photographed by Therese, November 2019.

www.ingramcontent.com/pod-product-compliance
Lightning Source LLC
Chambersburg PA
CBHW062048290426
44109CB00027B/2764